Aaron has a unique way [...] [...]ng through humor, personal experience, and biblical insight. In *Don't Miss Your Life*, he exposes the emptiness and deceptiveness of our pursuit of success. In the end, you're left with a compelling decision to change course.

Tom Petersburg, president, Catapult Ministries;
former chaplain, Cleveland Browns,
Cleveland Indians, and Cleveland Cavaliers

You are meant to be here. Yes, holding this book...but also here on earth. The problem is that too many people miss their purpose or don't know how to uncover it. This book can help! Aaron takes you on a fun, inspirational, story-filled journey that will give you tangible and practical next steps to help you move toward your best life. I am excited for you!

Ben Snyder, lead pastor, CedarCreek Church

In the athletic world, I've experienced what Aaron describes in *Don't Miss Your Life*: a life lived in pursuit of success, which only leads to emptiness. This book has given me practical steps to live for significance that glorifies God.

Travis Hafner, former Major League Baseball player
(17-year career)

Everyone has a story, a gift, a purpose…and a target. Aaron clearly and directly challenges you to question your target in life. *Don't Miss Your Life* will challenge you to evaluate what your identity is anchored in and evaluate how you are using your time, talent, and treasure. If your life feels less than full, this book illustrates grounded truths to provide a pathway toward significance.

Marshall Croom, retired CFO, Lowe's Companies, Inc.

Struggling on the treadmill of success? Searching for significance in all the wrong places? *Don't Miss Your Life* has the secret to discovering and redefining success and significance in a world that fills us with false hope. As a former professional athlete, I've been to the top of my profession only to have it all seemingly taken away. I've also experienced the same in business and in my family life. Those peaks and valleys can lure and deceive the best of us into a repetitive cycle that never ends. *Don't Miss Your Life* will point you to the answer you've been looking for: the abundant life Jesus has to offer. Aaron's winsome truth telling will capture your heart and mind in a unique way, spur you to evaluate your life, and encourage you to make the necessary changes that lead to true significance!

Steve Shak, managing director, Northwestern Mutual;
former number one draft pick, Major League Soccer

Have you ever felt empty no matter how hard you work, strive, or push? Maybe you have just reached the top. Maybe you are just beginning your journey and have yet to experience the feelings of never being satisfied. No matter what stage you are at, it's not too late to aim at the right target. In *Don't Miss Your Life*, Aaron will guide you to your true purpose in life and help you reassess your vision of success. You will discover the real reason you are on this earth and the overwhelming fullness you can feel when your target aligns with Jesus' target for your life. You will enjoy this book and find the target that God put you on earth to hit. Trust me. You won't be disappointed.

Christopher Hodgson, president, Driftwood Restaurants
and Catering

At some point, we all figure out that success doesn't satisfy our deepest desires. Discovering your purpose and living this out will bring you true fulfillment. Read this book and find out how to live your best life.

Christian Taylor, professional athlete;
two-time Olympic Gold Medalist

Don't Miss Your Life:

The Secret to Significance

Aaron Tredway

BroadStreet Publishing® Group, LLC
Savage, Minnesota, USA
BroadStreetPublishing.com

Don't Miss Your Life: The Secret to Significance

978-1-4245-6422-4 (softcover)
978-1-4245-6423-1 (ebook)

Stock or custom editions of BroadStreet Publishing titles may be purchased in bulk for educational, business, ministry, fundraising, or sales promotional use. For information, please email orders@broadstreetpublishing.com.

Typesetting by Garborg Design Works | garborgdesign.com
Cover by Ashley Owen
Interior graphics by Chris Brice

Printed in China
22 23 24 25 26 5 4 3 2 1

For my friend Bob,
who taught many to live a significant life.

The thief comes only to steal and kill and destroy; I have come that they may have life, and have it to the full.

—Jesus (John 10:10 NIV)

Table of Contents

Prologue

The Sin of Success:
An Autobiography

I never want to be a pastor, missionary, or speak in public. Those are my conditions. That was my first prayer. On the floor. In my dorm room as a college freshman.

Have you ever tried to make a deal with God?

How'd that work out for you?

It wasn't my best idea. Three years later someone called me. It wasn't God. It might as well have been.

"Hello, is this Aaron?"

"Yes," I say.

"Is this Aaron Tredway, the professional soccer player?"

"Yes," I say…with pride.

It had always been my dream.

When I was five years old, my dad came home from work one day; he said we were going to play a new game. He never played himself. I don't think he ever saw it played until that day in the park.

Remember orange slices and lukewarm Capri Sun? Anyone? Maybe you also grew up in the '80s?

Prologue

That day in the park I clearly saw my purpose. I jumped out of my dad's 1979 Datsun Bluebird, and I stood at the edge of the field. Fluorescent yellow socks pulled up to mid-thigh. White plastic pleather cleats. I was 44.5 pounds soaking wet. I'm certain the other kids were intimidated.

They were all running. They were all screaming. They were all chasing a ball but mostly just kicking each other. In that moment, I look up at my dad and his fantastic mustache. "I'm going to be a professional soccer player!" I say. I'm told that wasn't my dad's plan; he loved baseball. Maybe I should have played baseball. Maybe then God wouldn't have had Mike call me that day.

◎ ◎ ◎

"Aaron, this is *Mike*," the voice says.

"Mike, great to hear from you," I say. "Do I know you?"

"Ummm. Well. Not really. But you should come to Africa to serve God with us."

Hmmm…

Let's think.

I never want to be a pastor, missionary, or speak in public…

I didn't think long.

"Mike, I'll pass," I say.

Three weeks later, I was in Harare, Zimbabwe.

Maybe you've had an experience like that—defining?

Life-altering? A total reframing of why you exist? Maybe it was an event for you. Maybe it was a specific moment in time. Maybe you picked up this book because you need a moment like that. I know I needed this moment.

From the day I stood on that soccer field when I was five years old, I had one goal for my life—to become a professional soccer player; but honestly, I didn't know what that meant when I was young. There was no professional soccer league in the United States. I had never watched soccer on TV, and I had never been to a game that I wasn't playing in myself. So, my vision wasn't robust…but it was specific.

I wanted to be famous.

I wanted to make lots of money.

I wanted to drive a Pontiac Firebird Trans Am. It had to be a *black* Pontiac Firebird Trans Am with a robotic artificially intelligent electronic computer module—I watched too much *Knight Rider* as a kid—thanks, Hasselhoff!

Here's the point: *success* was my goal.

Jesus once asked an interesting question: "What good would it do to get everything you want and lose you, the real you?"[1]

Have you ever thought about that?

Have you ever gotten something you really wanted? Do

you remember how long you were *satisfied* until you wanted something else?

Soccer was like that for me.

I spent my life chasing, and working, and grinding, and hoping one day I would "make it." I actually slept with a soccer ball under my pillow most nights. I guess that explains my alignment issues. But I had a goal. And it wasn't just a goal—it was my target—the aim of my life.

That's why I set parameters with God. That night when I prayed for the very first time, I told God my *conditions*. "I'm willing to commit, to sacrifice, to follow Jesus" as long as "I never have to be a pastor, missionary, or speak in public."

I've noticed that God doesn't always honor back-alley deals, but he always has a plan. That's how I got to Africa. That's how I ended up on a dirt field with Mike, who pursued me until I agreed to go. I'll never forget the day.

The night before, we had played in a huge stadium in front of thousands of people, but now we were in the absolute middle-of-nowhere Africa—think mud huts, grass skirts, and kids with no clothes covered in dirt.

Carlos, my friend who played for the LA Galaxy, leans over to me as we're sitting there on the bus in the heat. "Why are *we* here?" he says. I had no idea.

There was no one in sight—no houses or huts or anything around. But there was a field full of rocks and glass. One end of the field appeared to be higher than the other. Significantly higher.

"Should we get off the bus?" Carlos says.

Neither of us moved.

◎ ◎ ◎

I've noticed it's hard to move when you don't know your purpose. It's even more difficult when your purpose leads you somewhere you didn't intend to go. Has that ever happened to you? Have you ever found yourself in a place or a circumstance you didn't anticipate? Maybe it's your current job. Maybe it's a relationship. Maybe it's this book.

That's how I felt as our coach walked off the team bus that day. "Watch this!" he says.

But nothing happened.

Same field. Same heat. Same desolate surroundings. But then everything changed. Kids started rushing the field. They were swinging in on vines. They were coming out of bushes. They were riding in on elephants—at least that's how I remember it—the moment our coach put a ball on the ground.

Did I mention the *clicking*?

Yeah, that's how they speak in Harare.

It's like, "Click, clock, clock, click…click, click." I think it means, "I really like your hair." It's TBD. But I have determined it's extremely difficult to communicate when clicking is your only option. That's why this moment was so profound.

I stood on the side of the field watching all the kids running and screaming and kicking each other, just like I did when I was five years old. Our players were running and screaming and kicking them too. We weren't clicking. They weren't speaking English. We were communicating, though, through soccer.

◎ ◎ ◎

Why am I here? What's my purpose? Why did I come to Africa? That's what I'm thinking as I'm standing there in the dirt watching the kids play. That's when our coach calls everyone together.

"Let's share Jesus!" Coach says.

Share? What? How? I'm totally confused. I knew we were in Africa to serve God, but what about the *clicking*? What about the cultural barriers? What about everything that separates us?

Maybe I should think more like a twelve-year-old sometimes. That's who shared Jesus that day—the coach's son.

It wasn't deep.

It wasn't complex.

It didn't have three points.

But Jesus was proclaimed. Hundreds of kids responded. The village chief was there. He committed his life to

Christ. A church was planted in the middle-of-nowhere Zimbabwe. Twenty years later, that church still exists. And I was there.

Standing on the side of the field. In the dirt. I watched it happen. God used my passion for his purpose, and it totally reframed my perspective of *success*.

◎ ◎ ◎

I always thought success was significant. That's the message we get from culture, at least. If you have the right degree, get the right job, hold the right position, make the right amount of money—you're good. If you gain fame, popularity, power, prestige—you're good. So… are you good? Is that how you *feel*? Satisfied? Fulfilled? Overflowing with *life*?

It's not how I *felt* for many years.

Maybe I was just too busy? Yes. That's it. I'm too *busy*! Schedule a vacation. A vacation will fix *everything*—marriage issues, anxiety, chronic stress, insomnia, diet, exercise, relationship with the kids—it's nothing five days and five nights on a beach won't fix.

Maybe I should take up yoga. Maybe I should rehearse daily self-affirmations. Maybe I should just drink more. Or…

Maybe the problem isn't the activity; it's the objective. Maybe I don't need to change what I'm doing; maybe I need to change *why* I do it.

That's what makes archery so intriguing to me. Remember archery circa high school gym class, and multiple teenagers who are legitimately given *weapons* they're ill-equipped to use? Yeah, it's an actual sport. It's characterized by a target—a series of concentric circles that represent a point value that increases as you move toward the center; it's called "the bull's-eye." That's the point. It's the goal. The objective of archery is to hit the *bull's-eye*.

I actually did that once—hit the bull's-eye. But my high school gym teacher, Mr. Stricker, said it didn't count. "What? It must count for something," I argued. "I hit the very center of the target!" Unfortunately, it wasn't *my* target. Maybe that's the problem in life.

Standing on the side of the field in Zimbabwe, I remembered a story I heard as a kid. I think God helped me remember. The story involves a girl named Esther and her cousin Mordecai.

Esther was a Jewish orphan raised by her cousin. When she was a teenager, she was "taken" and entered into a beauty pageant. I guess I always assumed Esther wanted to become queen of Persia, but as it turns out, she was actually forced into the position. The story has it all: beautiful girl, tyrant king, evil villain who wants to irradicate all the people. The watershed moment comes when Mordecai writes Esther a letter.

"Who knows but that you have come to royal position for such a time as this?"[2]

That's Mordecai's question to Esther. Do you think it's possible? Do you think there's a reason? Could it be that, *maybe, possibly, perhaps* there's a *purpose* for your life that's bigger than you can see?

Standing on the side of the field in Zimbabwe, I believed God was asking me the same question: *What's the point of all your striving? What's the goal of all your grinding? What's the target? What metric guides your life?*

I started to think about all the time I spent in the gym, on the field, late nights, early mornings, sacrifice, blood, sweat, pain... *What's the point? Money? Fame? Acceptance? Approval? I love to play soccer, but is there something* more?

Maybe success isn't as significant *as I think? Maybe success isn't the right goal?* Time stood still as I wrestled with all these questions in my mind.

I wonder if you've ever paused long enough to consider something more than success as the target of your life. Have you ever really considered if success can satisfy you? Can success fulfill you? Is success worth the price of admission? I'm not saying it's not. I just wonder if there's something more...*significant.*

◎ ◎ ◎

It's 4:27 a.m. Right now. As I type these words. I woke up at 3:45 a.m. because I have a goal: *finish the chapter.* That's what I wrote on my "to-do" list for today. I guess I'm type A? I don't like stereotypes. But I like setting goals. I like accomplishing goals even more.

Maybe you're like me. Just a little? Don't be ashamed. People use words like *determined* and *dedicated* and *passionate* to describe you. You take pride in doing whatever you do to the best of your ability. You work…a lot. Maybe it's schoolwork. Maybe it's your job. Maybe it's a passion you hope becomes a profession.

I used to think I needed to change who I am to live for God; now I know God made me like I am, so I just need the right target for my life.

It's like archery. The objective is to hit the bull's-eye; it's the point of the game. But I've always found it interesting that there's a term used in archery whenever you miss the mark of perfection. Any guesses? What could they possibly call it if you aim at the target but miss the point? It's called… *sin*. Look it up.

◎ ◎ ◎

Standing there, on the side of the field, I had this thought: *I've* sinned—*I totally missed the point of life.*

I thought life was all about me—my wants, my needs, my desires, my pursuits. I thought life was all about *success.* That was my metric. Success was my goal. Success was the measuring stick of my life. It's how I charted my progress. It's how I determined my emotions. Success was my greatest pursuit. But what if success is the wrong target? What if I aim at success and I'm successful but I miss my life?

I wonder if you've ever asked a similar question. Have you ever thought you might get everything you want but fulfillment? But joy? But satisfaction? What value do you place on actually enjoying the journey of life?

D. L. Moody once said: "Our greatest fear should not be of failure, but of succeeding at something that doesn't really matter."[3] Are there any things like that in your life? Are there any things you're pursuing, doing, spending lots of time thinking about, that don't really matter?

See, maybe success is significant. And maybe success is worth pursuing, but standing there in the dirt, I start to believe…

Significance is success.

I'm convinced this is the secret to life.

◎ ◎ ◎

I don't know about you, but I don't want to just get by. I don't want to just make it through, keep my fingers crossed, grit my teeth, work super hard to hopefully someday, somehow, with some luck limp across the finish line of life. That's not actually *life*. At least, not the life Jesus describes. Jesus says, "The thief comes only to steal and kill and destroy; I have come that they may have life, and have it to the full."[4]

I've decided, that's my goal—*life to the full*—it's the Jesus life. It's called "abundant."[5] It's called "rich and satisfying."[6] The Jesus life is called "real and eternal" *life*.[7] The problem is, so many of us miss the mark. Because we aim at the wrong target. Because we spend the bulk of our time, talents, and treasure pursuing the wrong objective.

I call it *the sin of success*.

It's not that success is bad. Success isn't wrong. But when success becomes our focus, we always miss the target.

So, what's the aim of your life? What's your *target*?

Maybe that's why you picked up this book. Maybe you're looking for a new metric to guide your life. Maybe you feel just a little like me. For so many years, in the back of my mind, I would think, *What's the point?*

"I never want to be a pastor, missionary, or speak in public." Those were my conditions. That was my first prayer. On the floor in my dorm room as a college freshman. Now I tell people, "Never make deals with God. He does whatever he wants."

I'm a pastor.

I was a missionary for twenty years.

I speak in public most days of the week.

But let me repeat the secret the world never told me: *significance is success*.

I've been practicing the secret to significance for over twenty-five years now. It doesn't mean I've cornered the market on life. I've got so much to learn. I make so many mistakes. I'm constantly aiming and re-aiming my trajectory. But life is different now.

I still have big dreams. I still set seemingly impossible goals. I literally want to climb mountains (I'm doing Everest next year), discover new places, and do things other people don't do.

I played professional soccer for thirteen years. I coached professional soccer teams on four continents. I even owned a professional soccer team…sort of. The point isn't really about what I've done or accomplished. The point is that you don't have to change your profession to fulfill your purpose. You just need to change your perspective and maybe your pursuit.

So, if success is your only concern, maybe skim the first chapter of this book and get back to it. But if *live to the full* sounds good to you, if you're tired of the chase, the grind, the endless pursuit of things that don't really matter or fulfill, if you've got a sneaking suspicion that *maybe, possibly, perhaps* there's a *purpose* for your life that's bigger than you can see, then keep reading.

This book isn't complex, and it's not hard to understand, but I'm guessing that, just like me, you don't want to miss your life. That's why we need to understand the secret to significance.

PART ONE:

The Problem

I think everybody should get rich and famous and do everything they ever dreamed of so they can see that it's not the answer.

—Jim Carrey

Chapter 1

SUCCESS: The Most Coveted Disappointment of All

A few years ago, I had coffee and crumpets with my friend Tim in the English countryside—it was a scene straight out of *The Crown* (season 1, of course; every other season is just average). Like every driven, overachieving, highly motivated person, Tim is *busy*. He's also fairly popular.

When we first met, Tim worked in a town called Manchester, and his work took him all over England, but Manchester was *home*. It's an interesting city, Manchester. For example—how do I say this—it's named after female anatomy. They say it has something to do with the Romans and a fort they built between two hills in AD 79.[8]

"Game day," Tim says, as I'm stuffing the last crumpet in my mouth.

"Game day?" I say.

"Yes, definitely game day," Tim says.

I guess I shouldn't have been surprised to find out that was Tim's *least* favorite day of the week—game day. At the time, Tim played for Manchester United. Talk about a high-pressure work environment. On any given weekend 1.35 billion…yes…*billion* people watch Manchester United play live.[9]

"So, you don't like game day?" I say.

"I love game day," Tim says. "It's my favorite day of the week."

"You just said it's your least favorite day of the week," I say.

"Yeah, that too," Tim says.

Have you ever noticed: *success* doesn't satisfy? It's like a big glass of water when you've been outside working in the yard on a really hot day, and you're dripping with sweat, and you're dehydrated, and your energy is almost gone… but the big glass of water is hot. It might be more like curry (come on, America, get on board…the rest of the world loves curry). Maybe you love curry. Maybe you can't wait to eat curry for dinner. Maybe curry is actually your favorite food, but it turns out that you love curry more than curry loves you. You know what I mean? I think you do.

Let me put it a different way: *success* is the most coveted disappointment of all.

"Prime Time," "Neon Deion" Sanders describes his experience with success in his book *Power, Money & Sex—How*

Success Almost Ruined My Life. Listen carefully to the only athlete to ever play in both the Super Bowl and the World Series. Sanders says, "I had all the material comforts and all the money and all the fame and popularity, but I had no peace…I had everything that power, money, and sex could give me, but it just wasn't enough…it didn't satisfy me. I realized I was empty inside. Desperately empty."[10]

But you won the Super Bowl—*twice*—Deion. You're in the NFL Hall of Fame. You have your own rap album. No peace? No satisfaction? Empty inside?

The late Kobe Bryant said something similar: "I have won and accomplished much. I own NBA championship rings. I've had plenty of endorsement deals and made a lot of money from them…But am I supposed to obsess myself with winning only to win, retire, and wonder if all my sacrifices were worth it?"[11]

That's an interesting thought: What is the value of success?

What's success worth to you? What are you willing to sacrifice? What are you willing to do to experience *success*?

Ever heard of the Goldman Dilemma?

In the 1980s, physician Robert Goldman began to survey elite athletes; he wanted to understand their mindset. He wanted to understand what an elite athlete would do to *win*. In his now famous research, here's the question Goldman posed:

> If I had a magic drug that was so fantastic that if
> you took it once you would win every competition
> you would enter from the Olympic Decathlon to the
> Mr. Universe, for the next five years, but it had one
> minor drawback—it would kill you five years after
> you took it—would you still take the drug?[12]

What would you do? Would *you* take the drug if it guaranteed you overwhelming success in business? In music? As a YouTuber? If you knew you would be the valedictorian of your class? If you were certain your company would become everything you've always dreamed it would be? Would you trade what you have to get what you want?

The question is: What are you willing to trade your life for?

What's the value of success?

It's the *Goldman Dilemma*.

Apparently, the majority of elite athletes would trade their *life* to *win*. Dr. Goldman's research found more than 50 percent of elite athletes would take the drug.

More recent research suggests 14 percent of Olympians would accept a fatal cardiovascular condition in exchange for Olympic Gold. I mean no offense, but it's…a medal. With some gold spray paint. With some string tied on it so it can hang around your neck. And it's not the majority, but I guess some people *are* "dying to win."

Consider Achilles.

Remember Homer? Not *Simpson*…the Mediterranean

one. The ancient Greek philosopher, Homer. He's like a Brazilian soccer player: one name is sufficient. He wrote two poems that are considered the foundational works of Greek literature—the *Iliad* and the *Odyssey*. Enter Achilles stage left.

In the *Iliad*, Homer's mythic warrior hero, Achilles, has a choice. It's the Goldman Dilemma…just 2,700 years early. Here's the choice: fight in the Trojan War and face imminent death but be remembered forever as a hero or return home to a long and happy life with loved ones and live in obscurity. Here's what Achilles says:

> Mother tells me…
>
> That two fates bear me on to the day of death.
>
> If I hold out here and I lay siege to Troy,
>
> my journey home is gone, but my glory never dies.
>
> If I voyage back to the fatherland I love,
>
> my pride, my glory dies.[13]

Let me translate with some simple math. Achilles decides:

My glory > my life.

Just like the majority of elite athletes, Achilles decides to take the drug. He'll accept the cardiovascular condition. He'll go to battle and die if glory is guaranteed. It might seem crazy. It might seem irresponsible. It might seem totally irrational. But just like modern-day philosopher 50 Cent says, "Success is my drug of choice."[14]

◎ ◎ ◎

The majority of us aim our lives at the target of success, not just athletes, Greeks, and the occasional rapper.

William James is called the "Father of American Psychology." James was the first educator to offer a psychology course at his alma mater, Harvard University. James once made this observation:

> We are not only gregarious animals, liking to be in sight of our fellows, but we have an innate propensity to get ourselves noticed, and noticed favorably, by our kind. No more fiendish punishment could be devised, were such a thing physically possible, than that one should be turned loose in society and remain absolutely unnoticed by all the members thereof. If no one turned round when we entered, answered when we spoke, or minded what we did, but if every person we met "cut us dead," and acted as if we were non-existing things, a kind of rage and impotent despair would ere long well up in us, from which the cruelest bodily tortures would be a relief; for these would make us feel that, however bad might be our plight, we had not sunk to such a depth as to be unworthy of attention at all.[15]

It's true. I want to be noticed, and so do you. It's part of our human condition. It's like C. S. Lewis says, "We should hardly dare to ask that any notice be taken of ourselves. But we pine. The sense that in this universe we are treated as strangers, the longing to be acknowledged, to meet with some response, to bridge some chasm that yawns between us and reality, is part of our inconsolable secret."[16]

I love it. It's classic Clive Staples...*our inconsolable secret...* we pine for attention. It's who we are. It's who *you* are. Don't believe me? When's the last time you touched your phone?

A recent study found that the average iPhone user touches his or her phone 2,617 times a day—that's roughly two and a half hours daily.[17] Millennials, it's twice as much for you. And maybe you aren't sitting on Snapchat all day, but all the research shows social media is designed to leverage our need for attention. It's like a *drug.*

According to a recent study by Harvard University, self-disclosure on social media lights up the same part of the brain that ignites when one is taking an addictive substance.[18] Here's how the Addiction Center describes it: "The reward area in the brain and its chemical messenger pathways affect decisions and sensations. When someone experiences something rewarding, or uses an addictive substance, neurons in the principal dopamine-producing areas in the brain are activated and dopamine levels rise. Therefore, the brain receives a 'reward' and associates the drug or activity with positive reinforcement."[19]

It turns out success works the same way. The more you have, the more you want. The more you want, the more you strive. The more you strive, the more you get. Then you want more.

It's called the hedonic treadmill.

◎ ◎ ◎

"I thought it would feel different," Greg says.

"*Different*?" I say.

"Yeah, I thought the day I finally had seven figures in my bank account I'd feel…," Greg pauses for dramatic effect, shrugs his shoulders, and says, "different."

Maybe you can relate? Maybe you've accomplished something or finished something or done something you really wanted to do, and it was *great*. You felt great. You were celebrated. You experienced a certain elation. But how did you feel three days later? Or maybe you rode the wave a for a while…three weeks? Three months? Three years?

I heard a sobering statistic at a conference a number of years ago—eight out of ten professional athletes in the United States will be one of three things within two years of retirement. Any guesses? Come on. Guessing games are fun…don't look down to the answer yet. What three things could 80 percent of all professional athletes *be* within two years of retirement?

1. Divorced

2. Bankrupt

3. In prison

How'd you do? How *successful* were you? (See what I did there?)

31

I was a professional athlete when I heard that statistic. I immediately assumed it could never happen to me. I think that's what we all assume. And you know what they say about *assumption*, right? Google it. Let's just say the odds weren't in my favor, and it has everything to do with the hedonic treadmill. Technically, it's called "hedonic adaptation." It's a psychological theory that first came to prominence in 1971.

Two psychologists, Brickman and Campbell, first wrote about this concept in their essay "Hedonic Relativism and Planning the Good Society."[20] It sounds really complex, but it's really not. Here's how I like to draw it (and I like to draw when I teach, which recently prompted a woman in my church to give me a book called *How to Draw Really Cute Stuff*—it's helping, I think):

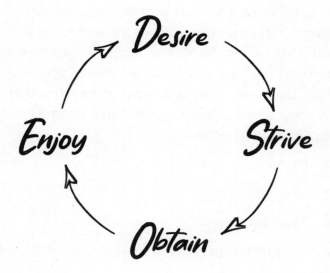

This is the hedonic treadmill. It's simple, right? We want something. So we begin to strive to get the thing we want. We obtain said thing. So we're happy; we enjoy that thing…for a while. Here's the problem: we *adapt* to our new reality with said thing.

Let's make it practical.

At present, 97 percent of Americans own a cell phone. That's up from 35 percent in 2011.[21] So, almost *everyone* has a phone. You might say it's a necessity. I think it's debatable. But we can agree, most people in the United States *want* a cell phone. So, this is a good example of hedonic adaptation. Here's the picture:

Do you see the problem here? When does it stop? When does it end? How do you get off the treadmill of desire?

It's a big problem if you happen to be breathing.

Jean-Jacques Rousseau explains the problem well in his 1754 *Discourse on Inequality*:

> Since these conveniences by becoming habitual had almost entirely ceased to be enjoyable, and at the same time degenerated into true needs, it became much more cruel to be deprived of them than to possess them was sweet, and men were unhappy to lose them without being happy to possess them.[22]

Even eighteenth-century philosophers know that, given time and familiarity, our *wants* become *needs*.

Shakespeare says something similar (not that I always understand what he says): "Happy thou art not, for what thou hast not, still thou striv'st to get, and what thou hast, forget'st."[23]

Got it? Thou striv'st. Thou get'st. Thou like'st. Thou forget'st.

This is the problem of aiming your life at the target of success—*happy thou art not*—for you always need something more.

◎ ◎ ◎

Do you know anxiety is the number one health issue for females in the United States today? Not cancer. Not heart disease. Not diabetes or high blood pressure. Anxiety. It's the number two health issue for men, just behind drugs and alcohol (which means it's probably number one for men since drugs and alcohol are often used to mask all the anxiety—just sayin'). Seventy percent of teenagers say anxiety is the number one issue they have in their life.[24]

There are many advantages to being American—many. Apparently mental health isn't one of them. The United States is the most *anxious* nation on earth by a long shot. Forty million people in America will deal with some form of anxiety that will disrupt their work, their families, and their lives over the next twelve months.[25] Spending on mental health treatment and services reached $225 billion in 2019,[26] and it's only getting worse.

You might say we're winning in worry. Maybe *you* are winning in worry?

For some of us, it's clinical—anxiety—you need clinical help. For the majority of us, it's circumstantial. I'm convinced the problem is the target of our life.

Former Formula One race car driver Alex Dias Ribeiro makes it clear:

> Unhappy is he who depends on success to be happy. For such a person, the end of a successful career is the end of the line. His destiny is to die of bitterness or to search for more success in other careers and to go on living from success to success until he falls dead. In this case, there will not be life after success.[27]

Many of us *bet the farm* on success (it's not just an expression. It originates from a guy who actually bet his family farm in a poker game in the Wild West). Maybe you don't have a family farm. But we build our life around the pursuit of success. We make decisions. We move to cities. We position all we have to achieve some *thing*. And maybe that's not why we're winning in worry. But maybe it is. Maybe that's why psychologists began studying lottery winners in 1978.

"Are lottery winners happier?" That's what researchers wanted to know. It seems obvious to me. It's like little Charlie Bucket in *Charlie and the Chocolate Factory*—he won the golden ticket. Everyone *wants* the golden ticket. But research reveals that the golden ticket doesn't shine forever. At least, that's what the study concluded in 1978. Here's their summary:

> Eventually, the thrill of winning the lottery will itself wear off. If all things are judged by the extent to which they depart from a baseline of past experience, gradually even the most positive events will cease to have impact as they themselves are absorbed into the new baseline against which further events are judged. Thus, as lottery winners become accustomed to the additional pleasures made possible by their new wealth, these pleasures should be experienced as less intense and should no longer contribute very much to their general level of happiness.[28]

It's the hedonic treadmill. Lottery winners are happy. Really happy. But it doesn't last. Within eighteen months, the majority of lottery winners return to whatever level of happiness they had prior to winning the lottery.[29]

It's applicable to both good stuff and bad stuff that happens in life. This illustration might help:

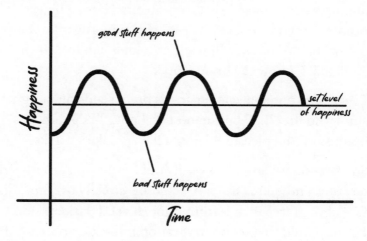

Have you experienced this? The thrill of victory and the agony of defeat both fade over time. So does the excitement of a new car. And the disappointment of a failed relationship. And the exhilaration of closing a deal. This is the problem of success as the target of life: it's the most coveted disappointment of all. No matter how high the high (and thankfully) how low the low, it's like Dostoyevsky says, "Yes, man is a pliable animal—he must be so defined—a being who gets accustomed to everything! That would be, perhaps, the best definition that could be given of him."[30] It's how the brain works.

I'm not a neuroscientist. I don't even own a white coat. I understand the brain has neural pathways though.

A neural pathway communicates information from one area of the nervous system to another. Here's a simple example—our son loves sugar (come on, who doesn't?). Our son is five. Much to our chagrin, our son eats copious amounts of sugar, and that's a problem. Here's a bigger problem: the more sugar he eats, the more sugar he wants. It's like he's *addicted*. Clinically speaking, I'm told, he *is* addicted. It's how the brain works.

Every time our son eats sugar, his brain sends out a signal similar to the "like" button on Facebook. "It's good!" his brain says. "It's pleasurable! 👍 Like. 👍 Like. 👍 Like."

So, we're on vacation last week, and I wake up abruptly on day one, and there's my son, standing directly over me, his face about three inches from mine. It's still dark outside. I've been told that it's not a vacation if the kid's present. It's a "family trip." I now agree.

Whispering (so as not to wake up the treat police sleeping next to me), he says, "Dad? Can you hear me?"

My eyes pop open.

"Dad? Can I have a treat now? A donut? Swedish Fish? Chocolate ice cream with rainbow sprinkles?" He's still whispering. It's 4:00 a.m. But he's *addicted*. He wants sugar. He feels he *needs* sugar.

"I don't negotiate with terrorists," I say. But he gets a donut at 8:00 a.m. And you might think that would satiate his desire? He got his fix. He's good. That's true. But every time our son has some sugar his brain says, "It's good! It's pleasurable! 👍Like. 👍Like. 👍Like. I want more!"

It's really a vicious cycle.

Nobel-prize winning psychologist Daniel Kahneman refers to this vicious cycle as a sort of "satisfaction tread-mill,"[31] where we continuously raise our standards once we reach our goals. It creates this need to be always striving. Always seeking. Always running after more…that is, if you want to feel *satisfied* again.

◎ ◎ ◎

The devil knows how the brain works. That's why he took Jesus to the top of a very high mountain and showed him how powerful he could be. The devil showed Jesus "the kingdoms of the world and their splendor."[32] He said, "It can all be yours!" Money. Fame. Approval. Power. The devil told Jesus he could have it all with one condition: "Bow down and worship me."[33]

What do you worship?

Jesus asks a significant question: "What will a man give in exchange for his life?"[34]

It sounds like a familiar question. It seems like lots of different people are asking the same question—you know—Greeks, rappers, psychologists, and such.

The question is: What are you willing to trade your life for?

I think Dr. Goldman was on to something. I think his research was groundbreaking; it's eye-opening. But there's a better name than the Goldman Dilemma:

The *Jesus Dilemma*.

See, Jesus says, "The thief comes only to steal and kill and destroy; I have come that they may have *life*, and have it to the full."[35]

I've heard some people...*pastors*...describe these words from Jesus as a threat. "There's an enemy trying to destroy you! There's a thief who wants to take from you! Beware!" they say. And I agree. We have an enemy. There *is* someone, or something, or some force that wants to hold us down and keep us from experiencing life, but it's really not a *threat*. It's an invitation to live for more.

Jesus invites you to experience *life*.

It's an invitation to get off the treadmill.

It's an invitation to take a breath.

It's an invitation to stop the constant running, chasing, striving, striving, striving, that so often characterizes life.

Doesn't that sound good?

◎ ◎ ◎

"I live for game day," Tim says.

I could relate.

For so long, for so many years, *game day* defined my life. I was a goalkeeper. I loved the pressure. I loved making the game winning save. But some days I didn't. Some days I was horrible. I'm just being honest. Some days I got paid to play soccer, but I didn't play well at all.

"You're the hero or the villain, right?" I say.

"Yup, there's no middle ground," Tim says.

It's just like a treadmill. You can change the speed. You can run faster. You can run slower. But unless you choose to get off the treadmill, you're always running.

That's the problem of success. No matter how much you have, you still want more. You feel you *need* more. You're never satisfied, no matter what you accomplish, no matter what you achieve. There's always the next deal. The next game. The next show. The next post. The next opinion. The next performance. The next sale.

It's like you're running on a treadmill. No matter what happens, it just keeps going, and going, and going. Maybe that works for you. Maybe treadmills are your thing. Maybe. But not me. I was a goalkeeper. I like jumping. I like catching. I like diving.

So, think: Are you tired of running? Anyone? Just a little?

If you could be happier, if you could be more fulfilled, if you could be more satisfied and still have success—would you want that?

Jesus says it's possible.

It's the secret to significance.

41

You don't have to keep running.

It's not a threat.

It's an invitation.

If that sounds good to you, keep reading.

Chapter 2

THE AMERICAN DREAM

"The target moved!" I shout.

"*What?*" Matt says. "No chance! You missed!"

"It definitely *moved*. Redo!" I say, smiling.

"*What?*" Matt says again. "There's no redo in this game!"

My friend Matt and I had this conversation…*last night*. The truth is, we have some version of this conversation almost every day. We like to compete. We like to test our abilities in matters of useless importance. Can you relate?

Here's the scene: we just finish another smackdown session of our favorite couples' game, *Sequence*. We're standing in the front yard. The kids are terrorizing each other. It's almost completely dark. Matt's twelve-year-old daughter is playing with a Hula-Hoop twenty yards away.

"I bet you can't kick a ball through that Hula-Hoop," Matt says.

"I will *definitely* kick a ball through that Hula-Hoop," I say.

Matt calls to his unsuspecting daughter, "Hey, Londyn, hold the Hula-Hoop above your head!"

◎ ◎ ◎

I've noticed that the pursuit of success is like trying to kick a soccer ball through a Hula-Hoop held by a twelve-year-old girl—the target often moves. Consider the research of Harvard Business School professors Laura Nash and Howard Stevenson. The pair surveyed hundreds of business professionals to understand the assumptions behind the idea of success. Here's their conclusion:

> Pursuing success is like shooting at a series of moving targets. Every time you hit one, five more pop up from another direction. Just when we've achieved one goal, we feel pressure to work harder to earn more money, exert more effort, possess more toys. Standards and examples of "making it" constantly shift, while a fast-paced world of technological and social change constantly poses new obstacles to overcome.[36]

To make it plain, the landscape of success *moves*, and that's a problem. It's experiential. It's also historical. Take the *American Dream*, for example. Do you know who created the idea? Do you know why the idea was birthed? What is the "American Dream"?

Let's think about it.

I wish we were sitting across from each other sipping our

favorite coffee drink right now. I've got a spot. There's a waterfall in the center of our town. They say people used to jump off the bridge into the rocky river below. I've never seen it happen. I've seen a lot of people sipping coffee though. Since we can't be there together, we'll have to do it this way.

Say someone comes up to you and wants to know, "What *is* the American Dream?" What would you say? And I never like to *pause* when I'm told to do so in a book. But I'll still make the request. Pause. Think. Write it down. How would you define the American Dream? I'll even give you a place to write.

The American Dream is: _____

_____

Here's how the *Oxford English Dictionary* defines the American Dream. And the irony isn't lost on me:

> The ideal that every citizen of the United States should have an equal opportunity to achieve success and prosperity through hard work, determination, and initiative.[37]

Is this definition anywhere close to your dream?

Equal opportunity.

Success.

Prosperity.

That's how the British describe the American Dream.

Consider a more *American* definition, "A happy way of living that is thought of by many Americans as something that can be achieved by anyone in the US especially by working hard and becoming successful."[38]

I like how that sounds. *A happy way of living*. It's the American Dream. Doesn't that sound good to you?

◎ ◎ ◎

Here's a serious question: Are you happy?

I know, you might be happier if I don't ask you to pause and reflect again. But I'll still make the request. Pause. Think. Write it down. It's a yes or no question. I'll even state it in the first person.

Am I happy? (*Remember*, yes or no) _____

According to the World Happiness Report, if you're American, and you're honest, you probably *aren't* happy. I wish I had better news. Actually, are you from The Land of a Thousand Lakes? Finnish friends, well done! You rank number one of the happiest people on the entire planet four years running.[39] Americans, not so much. According to the report—we're not even in the top ten!

Two-thirds of Americans claim to be unhappy.[40]

When I read that, I immediately thought, "The World Happiness Report is wrong." No offense, Finland. But maybe most Americans misunderstood the question. We are really *busy* as a nation, after all. Maybe we just rushed through the answers.

Are you happy?

It seems straightforward. It seems obvious. But how could 66.66 percent of Americans really be *unhappy*? We're the most prosperous nation in the world. We have one of the highest standards of living. We have Pharrell. We must be happy. But the numbers don't lie, and the problem is, they're incongruent with the American Dream. It's also incongruent with the life Jesus says he came to bring.

One thousand seven hundred and seventy-six years after Jesus came offering life to the full, some guys signed a document at the Pennsylvania State House. It was a pretty big deal then. It's still a big deal. The document they signed on August 2, 1776, is, of course, the Declaration of Independence.

You might remember the five guys tasked with drafting the formal statement to justify the thirteen North American colonies departure from Great Britain: Thomas Jefferson, Ben Franklin, John Adams, Roger Sherman, and Robert Livingston. I'll be honest; I had to look them up. I've never been great at remembering historical names or dates. I've always remembered these words though:

> We hold these truths to be self-evident, that all men are created equal, that they are endowed by their Creator with certain unalienable Rights, that among these are Life, Liberty and the pursuit of Happiness.

These are the words of America's Founding Fathers. Thomas Jefferson wrote the first draft. There were eighty-six revisions thereafter.

These words embody the philosophy of what it means to be American—a nation founded with "certain *unalienable* Rights." Have you noticed, they aren't called unalienable hopes or dreams or desires or beliefs? In America, they are *rights*.

Americans have the right to life.

Americans have the right to liberty.

Americans have the right to the pursuit of happiness.

These are *rights*.

The Founding Fathers designed the Declaration of Independence knowing their actions, under British law, could result in death by hanging, but John Adams called it "the most memorable epocha in the history of America."[41] Thomas Jefferson would pray that "the annual return of the day forever refresh our recollections of these rights, and an undiminished devotion to them."[42]

The words of the Declaration of Independence clearly had meaning to the Founding Fathers of America. They were written and revised, and written and revised, ad nauseum. It's almost like these men believed their words would influence the fabric of American life *forever*. Like these words would serve as a guide: a true north. Like these ideals would be the target.

Some might say the Founding Fathers of America had a *dream*. They didn't name it at the time, but a century and a half later, someone called it the *American Dream*.

It's a dream for everyone, at all times; not just five guys who signed a document at the Pennsylvania State House in 1776.

It makes me think of my grandmother.

My grandmother is ninety-nine years, eight months, and twenty-seven days old…*today*. Less than a year ago she moved for the first time in sixty-nine years. She didn't have to move, but her dating life was hindered because most ninety-nine-year-old men can't drive. She's closer to the action now. Take that as you will.

My grandmother's name is Miyoko Yamadera. Her maiden name was Hayashi. Her parents were born in the United States. Her parents' parents were born in Japan. I called her the other day.

"*Bachan* (Japanese for "grandma"), what is the American Dream?" I say.

Silence. Crickets. No response.

"*Bachan*, are you there?" I yell into the phone.

"Oh, sorry, dear, I was watching my show," Bachan says.

She's actually still sharp as a tack. She's a keen gambler too—organizes a monthly bus trip to Reno, Nevada, for all her Japanese friends to play the nickel slots.

I decide to ask the question again, with context this time. Now speaking slightly louder...

"*Bachan*, I'm writing a new book, and I need your help. Tell me what you think the American Dream is?" I say.

"*Ohhhhhhhh...*" (picture Mr. Miyagi's voice from *Karate Kid 1*, the scene where he's had too much Sake to drink) "Ok, ok," she says. "I see. *America* Dream."

Long period of silence.

"Opportunity!" Bachan finally says. "The America Dream is *opportunity*."

◎ ◎ ◎

After ninety-nine years, eight months, and twenty-seven days, I think Bachan remembers something many of us have forgotten. The American Dream began as a declaration of *opportunity*, not a promise of personal success. The Founding Fathers dreamed of a nation free to pursue life to the full; their vision was for a social order in which every citizen could attain the best of which they were capable, equally. But something changed. It's actually how the term *American Dream* came to be.

Ever heard of James Truslow Adams?

A historian by trade, Adams is credited with popularizing the term *American Dream* in his 1931 book *The Epic of America*. Apparently, the book was Adams' attempt to save the "priceless heritage" of America, as he put it.[43]

Until 1931 the American Dream was an ideal; it was a set of ideas that served as a guide for America, but Adams says the Great Depression caused a shift in perspective. The economic and political instability of the day introduced a new mindset, one that prized material success above all other values. Instead of treating money as a means to produce value, Adams says, "Material success became a good in itself."[44]

Listen carefully to Adams' declaration of the American Dream:

> It's not a dream of motor cars and high wages merely, but a dream of social order in which each man and each woman shall be able to attain to the fullest stature of which they are innately capable, and be recognized by others for what they are, regardless of the fortuitous circumstances of birth or position.[45]

For Adams, the American Dream was a vision of "commonweal."[46] It means common well-being. It means common welfare. It means common good.

This was the dream of the Founding Fathers of America. They believed in it. They wrote it down. They lived it out. But things are different now. The target shifted. The vision changed. And it's possible no one told you.

◎ ◎ ◎

So, what does this brief history of the United States have to do with me? Is that what you're thinking? Just a little? It's ok. I started thinking that a few pages ago myself.

Here's the point: material success was never the goal, but it might be yours. Think about it. The implications are profound.

James Truslow Adams does well to state the problem of success as our goal. He notes, "How we forgot to *live* in the struggle to 'make a living.'"[47]

Do you ever feel like that? Do you ever wonder if you're actually *living* life? I like how John Ortberg sums it up:

> For many of us the great danger is not that we will renounce our faith. It is that we will become so distracted and rushed and preoccupied that we will settle for a mediocre version of it. We will just skim our lives instead of actually living them.[48]

When I first read that I almost fell off my chair. Literally. Did that just happen to you? Be honest. Like I said, the implications of success as our goal are profound. Maybe that's why so many of us are unhappy? Maybe that's why *you* are unhappy?

Are you skimming your life or living it?

It's the challenge of hedonic adaptation. Remember the treadmill?

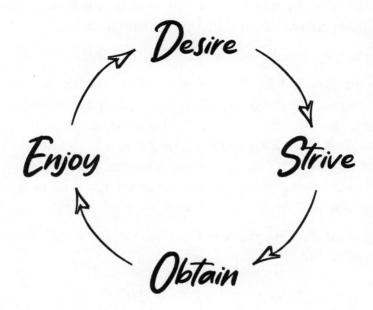

The problem of success as our goal is that we're never satisfied. I might have said that before. I'll say it again… at least twice. Success doesn't satisfy. Did you underline it? Circle it? Tattoo it on your forearm in Latin? *Success doesn't satisfy*. It doesn't impact our long-term happiness either; that's what the professionals say.

Psychologists say you have a personal happiness baseline. It's inherent. It's fixed. It's impenetrable. So, here's the good news: no matter what happens in your life you will return to your personal happiness baseline. Here's the bad news: no matter what happens, you return to your personal happiness baseline.

That's what psychologists say: happiness is a predetermined condition that fluctuates circumstantially, for a time.

Jesus says something different.

In his most famous sermon, Jesus explicitly addresses happiness. Here's the word Jesus uses—*blessed*. It means fortunate, abundant, or blissful. *Blessed* means happy. If you're like me, you're thinking, "Yes! Sign me up! I want to be blessed!" It's like the person who says, "Can I pray for you?" Here's my response, *every time*: "Yes! Absolutely! Pray for me!" To say no is not even a consideration.

Jesus speaks of *happiness* in a similar way. There's only one small caveat. Here's what Jesus says:

> Blessed/Happy are the poor in spirit…
>
> Blessed/Happy are those who mourn…
>
> Blessed/Happy are the meek…
>
> Blessed/Happy are those who hunger and thirst for righteousness…
>
> Blessed/Happy are the merciful…
>
> Blessed/Happy are the pure in heart…
>
> Blessed/Happy are the peacemakers…
>
> Blessed/Happy are those who are persecuted because of righteousness…[49]

So, hands up. Who wants to be *happy*?

Are you meek? Are you merciful? Are you pure in heart? Do you seek peace? Do you hunger and thirst for righteousness? Jesus says these characteristics are the secret to happiness.

I preached a sermon series on this once. I played a little game on social media in preparation. Maybe you've played? It's called "Would You Rather?" It happens to be one of my favorite games.

Would you rather…have chronic, repulsive halitosis or flipper-feet?

Would you rather…have a small horn on your forehead or neigh like a horse whenever you laugh?

Sorry. It's a really fun game.

Here's the question I asked about the Sermon on the Mount: Would you rather be (a) poor, hungry, and persecuted or (b) rich, fat, and celebrated?

It's interesting—no one *liked* option *a*. Not even C. S. Lewis, I'm guessing.

Reflecting on Jesus' instruction in the Sermon on the Mount, Lewis once said, "As to 'caring for' the Sermon on the Mount, if 'caring for' means 'liking' or 'enjoying,' I suppose no one at all would 'care for' it. After all, who can like being knocked flat on his face by a sledge-hammer?"[50] Maybe that's how the pursuit of happiness feels to you? Two steps forward, five steps back. Like every time you begin to summit the elusive peak of happiness, you're struck down by the proverbial *sledge-hammer* to the face.

Could that be the point? In the most famous sermon Jesus would preach, could Jesus be trying to reframe our understanding of how to be happy? Here's what the psalmist says, "You will show me the path of life; In Your presence is fullness of joy; At Your right hand are pleasures forevermore."[51]

That seems like a promise to me. God intends for us to enjoy life. God wants us to be fulfilled, satisfied, quenched...*happy*. Throw in whatever adjective you'd like, God's plans for us are *good*. The problem is, somewhere along the way we lost sight of the target. Maybe we forgot the dream. Maybe we never knew the dream? But the problem is clear.

The pursuit of success is like trying to kick a soccer ball through a Hula-Hoop held by a twelve-year-old girl—it's fickle at best.

The pursuit of success is not illegal.

It's not unethical.

It's not unchristian.

But the pursuit of success for the purpose of success alone is not the American Dream. It's not God's dream for you either.

Chapter 3

THE SISYPHEAN EFFECT

Here's how the story goes: Sisyphus is king of Corinth. He's the son of Aeolus—ruler of the winds. His name means *crafty* in Greek—you could add words like wily, sly, cunning or devious…they all work…that's what he was. In Greek folklore, Sisyphus is the master trickster. It's his calling card; it was also his downfall. Sisyphus cheated death—*twice*. Apparently, the Greek gods weren't happy. Remember Zeus, the guy always holding the thunderbolt? He actually takes Sisyphus by the collar and drags him to an eternal punishment: rolling a stone up the hill. That's it.

Would you choose to be Sisyphus?

It might not be so bad, rolling a stone up a hill. I've done CrossFit a few times. I've climbed Mt. Kilimanjaro—The Roof of Africa. If you're feeling sporty, you might think, *bring it*!

But here's the problem for Sisyphus; it's our problem, too, whenever our life is aimed at the wrong target:

The summit never comes.

Whenever Sisyphus gets close to the top, the rock rolls. Whenever Sisyphus starts to think, *I'm almost there. I can taste it. I can feel it. I'm gonna make it!* The end eludes him. The finish line turns out to be a fable. It's the unenviable punishment the gods issue Sisyphus—push the rock to the top of the mountain. The only problem is that it is impossible to get to the top.

It's the Sisyphean Effect. Think of it as an impossible task.

Maybe you've experienced this. Maybe, like me, you've thought things like, *When I finish* _____, *then I'll* _____. *When* I close this deal. *When* I sell this house. *When* I finish this degree. *When* I get over this loss. *Then* I will rest. *Then* I will take a vacation. *Then* I will invest in the relationship. *Then* I will feel different than I feel now.

Do you ever think like this? *When/Then*? You might need to think about it.

I'm guessing it's how Sisyphus thought. Why else would he keep pushing the same rock up the same mountain? Why would he keep going day after day, *forever*? Why wouldn't Sisyphus just sit down one day and acknowledge that the summit won't arrive—it's an impossible task?

Maybe it's why they call doing the same thing over and over and expecting a different result *insanity*. Not to be confused with *Linsanity*.[52] But I think they are on to something. Whoever *they* are.

It's the problem of *when/then* thinking. It never ends. It's… *insanity*. We just keep thinking *when/then*, *when/then*, *when/then*, but *when* the thing you want finally happens, *then* another *when* pops up.

Have you experienced this?

I like how Solomon put it. The Bible calls him the wisest man to ever live. He was a king, just like Sisyphus. Solomon says, "Human desire is never satisfied."[53]

It's an interesting conclusion for a man who made the equivalent of one billion dollars a year (roughly the amount of 666 talents at the present value of gold).[54] The guy had it all—money, power, fame, public approval. He'll tell you: he got whatever he wanted. But he could never get enough. Here's what Solomon says reflecting on his life:

> I did great things:
>
> built houses, planted vineyards, designed gardens and parks and planted a variety of fruit trees in them, made pools of water to irrigate the groves of trees…
>
> then I acquired large herds and flocks…
>
> I piled up silver and gold, loot from kings and kingdoms.
>
> I gathered a chorus of singers to entertain me with song,
>
> and—most exquisite of all pleasures—
>
> voluptuous maidens for my bed…

Everything I wanted I took—I never said no
to myself. I gave in to every impulse, held back
nothing…

Then I took a good look at everything I'd done,
looked at all the sweat and hard work. But when I
looked, I saw nothing but smoke. Smoke and spitting into the wind. There was nothing to any of it.
Nothing.[55]

I've never walked in Solomon's shoes, but "smoke and
spitting into the wind" don't seem like the ingredients of
an enjoyable life. Maybe it depends on where you're from.
I've noticed some people really like spitting.

Nineteenth-century political economist Henry George
said something similar to Solomon, "Man…is the only
animal whose desires increase as they are fed; the only animal that is never satisfied."[56]

Maybe for you it's the unending pile of laundry? Yard
work? Kids' behavior? Home improvements? I can keep
going. The problem is that so often we think *when/
then*, but *then* never comes. It's the Sisyphean Effect.
No matter what the task, we think, *Eventually, I'll get
there. Eventually, I'll make it. Eventually, my thirst will be
quenched. My need will be met. My itch*…well, you get it.
The problem is, it's an impossible task. Whenever you aim
at the wrong target, that is.

◎ ◎ ◎

I don't know about you, but when I hear stories about guys like Sisyphus, I'm generally unfazed. *Uninterested* is more accurate. I have this ongoing debate with my friend Joe about Harry Potter and Bilbo Baggins being brothers. Honestly, all those guys are the same to me. They fit into one category in my brain—*fantasy*. And I'm not a fan of fantasy. But Sisyphus became real one day during a phone call with my mom.

"Can I throw away those two big boxes in the garage?" Mom says.

"Boxes…um…I don't know," I say. I haven't lived at my parents' house since 1994.

"Well, tell me if you want them because I already put them in the trash," Mom says.

I think for a second, then say, "If you already put them in the trash, why did you call?"

"Courtesy," says Mom.

Have you had an experience like this? One that seems insignificant but significantly shifts your perspective? It doesn't happen every day, but this was one of those times for me. I called Mom again the next week.

"Hey! Did you ever look in those boxes of mine you threw in the trash?" I ask.

"Oh…the garbage man picked those up yesterday. Don't

worry," Mom says. "There was nothing important in them. Just some stuffed animals and a bunch of trophies."

"*Trophies*?" I ask.

"That's right," Mom says casually. Then she hangs up the phone.

Honestly, I hadn't thought about those trophies in twenty-five years, but the thought of my entire youth sports career now in residence at the municipal landfill *irked* me. I wasn't mad at Mom. I was mad at myself. Those trophies were *life* to me growing up. Now they were in the trash.

I wonder, do you ever spend your life working for things that have limited value?

I'm not talking about things that must get done—paying bills, walking the dog, changing diapers—stuff everyone *must* do. I'm talking about spending your *life*—time, talent, treasure—on stuff that offers minimal return on investment. At least, ROI that lasts. That's what those trophies were for me.

When I was seven years old my best friend and I made a bet: who could win the most trophies by the day we graduated from high school. At the time, my allowance was twenty-five cents a week, so we bet the most money we could imagine—twenty dollars! It wasn't about the money. Trust me. I don't know what it was about, actually. I just know I wanted *more trophies* than my friend. That's how I defined success.

Maybe you've pursued a goal like that. Maybe you

accomplished the goal. Maybe you got everything you hoped you would get. But what was your *next* thought? What was your next desire? Retire to an island paradise? Live out your days off-the-grid on a Montana homestead? No more worry? No more fear? No more…well, what was your next thought?

I remember the day I won the trophy competition. After eleven years of sacrifice, suffering, hard work, and pain, *I won*. I went to my friend's house. I had a huge grin on my face. I stuck out my hand and said, "Pay up, buddy!" And he did. I won the greatest competition of my youth. I received the reward. And it felt good. No, it felt great! It felt like *success*. The only thing is, twenty-five years later, all my success was now in the trash.

◎ ◎ ◎

Here's how people who are much smarter than I am define success: the attainment of wealth, position, honors, or the like.[57] In British English they include the word *fame*. Gen Z likes to include that word too. Just sayin'.

Success is defined by other words like—*achievement, acquisition, high-rank, high-position, winner, triumph, prosperity, profit* and *a favorable outcome*. Any of those appeal to you? Any of those things seem like a worthy pursuit? Be honest. I won't blame you if they do. We live in a success-based culture: it's who we are; it's what we do. It's like that thing Jesus says about being salt and light. It's obvious:

Salt exists to be salty; light is supposed to shine. It's what they are; it's what they do.

I'll try to be clear on this point: Wealth, position, honors, or the like—none of these things are the problem. Achievement: not a problem. Acquisition: not a problem. All the other words used to describe *success*: not a problem. It's just like having money is not a problem. The problem is when *money* has *you*.

This *is* the problem with the pursuit of success: success can be the all-consuming, never-ending, impossible task.

It's easy to think, *Just one more win. One more trophy. One more promotion. One more deal. One more sale. One more trip up the mountain.* The problem is that the end never comes; the finish line is a fable.

It's the Sisyphean Effect.

Listen to how Albert Camus describes it in his insightful essay *The Myth of Sisyphus*:

> Sisyphus is the absurd hero. He is, as much through his passions as through his torture. His scorn of the gods, his hatred of death, and his passion for life won him that unspeakable penalty in which the whole being is exerted toward accomplishing nothing. This is the price that must be paid for the passions of this earth.[58]

Remember Solomon? I think this is what he's saying: human desire is never satisfied. But we still try. Just like

Sisyphus, we keep going. We keep pursuing. We keep striving, and working, and grinding toward a goal that will never fully arrive.

It's like CycleBar.

My wife and I recently got into indoor cycling. Apparently, it's not called *spinning* anymore. At least not at CycleBar. I was corrected at the door.

"Welcome to CycleBar!" says the over-caffeinated twentysomething in a one-piece spandex jumpsuit. I'm happy, but I'm not *that happy* at six in the morning.

"Thanks?" I say.

Now speaking at advanced auctioneer level, Twentysomething says, "We're so glad you're here. Fill this out. Check this box. Take this form. Sign this waiver. Drop to the floor and give me thirty." Ok, we didn't do pushups. But it was a lot for so early in the day.

"Ginny, you're on bike ten. Aaron, you're on bike thirteen. Have *so much fun*!" Twentysomething says.

It's dark. The music is loud. The class is starting.

"What bike did she say I'm on?" I ask Ginny.

"I don't think it matters," Ginny says. Apparently, it does matter. Ten minutes into the class, the instructor reveals the real-time standings. Every rider is ranked in order, according to some equation of speed, power, and calorie-burn. From my perspective, it doesn't matter what the factors are, as long as I'm in first place.

After ten minutes, I was in last.

Internal dialogue of a former professional athlete now in his mid-forties: *Whaaaaaat?* I sat in that thought for a moment. Self-talk ensues. It might have been audible, I'm not sure. *Come on, Aaron! You're an athlete! Pull it together! Work harder!* So, I do…*work harder.* For the next twenty minutes, I'm all in. Pedal to the metal. Sweat flowing. Legs burning. Breath limited. The instructor puts the standings back on the screen. Here's the image as I recall:

1. *Ginny Tredway*
2. Fred Smith
3. John Doe
4. Any name works
5. Any name works
6. Any name works
7. Any name works
8. Any name works
9. Any name works
10. Any name works
11. Any name works
12. Any name works
13. Any name works
14. *Aaron Tredway*

There are now ten minutes left in the class. There's only one option in my mind. *Work even harder.* So, I do. Right to the end of the class. I give it everything. I still finish last.

"Wasn't that fun?" Ginny says as the lights come on. She finished *first* by a country mile.

"Um, not really," I say. "I don't think I'm built for indoor cycling." Honestly, I probably would have never done another class if Twentysomething hadn't mentioned this as we walked out the door: "I had you on the wrong bikes," Twentysomething says. "Ginny, you were actually bike thirteen. Aaron, you were bike ten."

◎ ◎ ◎

I'm guessing you have the ability to work hard, especially when the chips are stacked against you. I've noticed this pattern in my life, whenever I'm not where I want to be or there's something I really want to accomplish, I just put my head down, shut out the distractions and *work*. It's not a bad attribute on its own. But when paired with the wrong target in life, it's deadly. At least for your soul it is.

Jesus once asked his disciples this brutally raw question: Is anything worth more than your soul?[59]

Anything?

On the surface, it's not a difficult question to answer. Right? I think the problem is that too often our head is down, our eyes are closed, and we're working to accomplish some goal, but we're actually missing our life. Even worse, we're trading away our soul. I've noticed it's never the plan though, to trade our soul. It's never the objective. It's never our goal. Think about a wedding day.

I get to perform weddings, and it's part of my job that I love. Two people stand before each other and God, and they pledge their undivided devotion, one to another. You might not believe in Jesus, but it's a sacred moment no matter who you are.

I've performed many weddings. I've stood with couples at the altar or the beach or the rooftop or the repurposed barn, which seems to be very popular these days. It doesn't really matter where you stand. On your wedding day, no one ever says, "I love you, *but*…one day we'll get divorced." It's never the plan. On their wedding day, no one ever thinks divorce is imminent. But it happens 50 percent of the time.

You don't plan to miss your life.

You don't plan to trade your soul.

But it happens.

Look at Sisyphus. He was clearly a talented guy. I'm guessing he was strong as well. There must be some benefit to eternally pushing a rock up a mountain. The question is, why didn't Sisyphus stop? Why did Sisyphus keep repeating the same task, the same way, day after day? We could speculate: it was hubris; it was stubbornness; it was persistence or tenacity. It's Greek mythology; we'll never know. But Sisyphus spent his life pursuing an impossible task. Is that what you want to do?

◎ ◎ ◎

Some people speculate that Sisyphus must have been addicted to success. It's an interesting theory. Especially when you consider a recent study conducted by the Harvard Graduate School of Education. According to a national survey of over ten thousand students, almost 80 percent of youth identify *individual achievement* as more important to them than having concern for others.[60] According to another study conducted with over forty thousand college students across multiple continents from 1989 to 2016, an overwhelming majority were found to have unrealistic expectations for personal achievement.[61]

Do these findings suggest addiction to success is a *thing*? Maybe. But they do suggest we have an unhealthy preoccupation with personal achievement. Psychologists are talking about it. Medical doctors are talking about it. Life coaches are talking about it. It is a thing. And no one has labeled it a *disease* yet, but that's where it's heading, based on the prevalence of depression, anxiety, loneliness, and the general dissatisfaction most of us feel.

Here's the problem: we tell our self, *I'm good.*

Do you ever say that? When you see a friend at the store.

"Hey, good to see you," they say. "How are you?"

"I'm good!"

Waiting for the diagnosis from your doctor.

Your spouse says, "Are you ok?"

"I'm good!"

Pressure is mounting at work, marriage feels rocky, kids are disengaged.

Your best friend calls to check in. "How's life?" they say.

"Um...well...hmmm...I'm good!"

I don't know about you, but I find it's hard to be honest about how I'm actually feeling sometimes. So, let's do a quick self-inventory. Remember, success is defined as the attainment of wealth, position, honors, or the like. The question is, how addicted to success are you? Here are my ten symptoms of what I call *success sickness*. Give yourself one point for any symptom that applies to you:

1. **Insecurity**: You work non-stop to satiate the feeling of not measuring up. It could be housework, school work, job work—you're in a constant state of motion, always feeling you need to prove your worth. You do more and more and *more*, but you *never* feel like you can do enough; it's never good enough; it's never perfect enough; it's never... enough. You always feel like you're being judged, like your life is under constant critique. You often compare yourself to those around you. _____

2. **Insomnia**: You are mentally and physically exhausted, but you can't fall asleep. When you do fall asleep, you never feel like you are actually sleeping. You often wake up in the middle of the night. You lie in bed thinking, pondering,

70

strategizing, replaying scenarios from the day. You regularly wake up tired. You are often grumpy, irritable, or curt because you aren't rested. _____

3. **Loneliness**: You feel successful but disconnected from God and others. You feel disconnected from your own soul. You have friends, but when you're with them, you feel a million miles away. You don't have enough time for a meaningful relationship with your spouse or your kids. You feel misunderstood, underappreciated. You're accomplishing your goals but feel like you're living life all by yourself because others can't relate to your aspirations. _____

4. **Dissatisfaction**: Happiness is temporal. Joy is minimal. You experience a "win," and you feel good when you do, but it doesn't last. The feeling of accomplishment fades quickly. You can't sustain a positive outlook. You have fun, but you carry a low-grade sense of emptiness in much of what you do. _____

5. **Workaholism**: You can't stop. You won't stop. You don't know how to stop. Another email. Another text. You extend visits to the bathroom to get one more email sent. You take pride in being the first person in the office each morning and the last one to leave. There's no day off. You take vacation but work most of the time. The first thing you do each morning is look at your phone. You want to spend

meaningful time with God and others, but you're too busy. _____

6. **Perfectionism**: It's all or nothing for you. You have unrealistic standards. You are often irrational in your goal setting. The bottom line is always your bottom line. You are driven by results. _____

7. **Burnout**: You can be irritable or impatient with coworkers, customers, or clients. Cynical is a word other people would use to describe you. You feel depressed. You find less or no joy doing things that used to bring fulfillment. You feel anxious more often than you don't. _____

8. **Addiction**: These could be called escapist behaviors—you turn to distractions like regularly binge-watching Netflix, excessive social media use, over-eating, over-drinking, watching porn—you name your drug of choice. Your activities aren't considered socially unacceptable, but you know they fail to feed your soul and you can't stop.

_____

9. **Risk-Taking**: I'm not talking about BASE jumping or swimming with sharks, but you find yourself taking unhealthy risks in order to reach your goals. You compromise your ethics for greater success. You think no one will know. You probably won't be found out, but you find yourself looking for short-cuts that will advance your cause, regardless of their moral implications. _____

10. **Imposter Syndrome**: You don't feel worthy of success. You question whether you deserve what you have. You fear others will discover you are a fraud despite your accomplishments. You feel insecure in your own skin. _____

So, how did you do?

I'm guessing the over-under on this little assessment is six or seven.

Maybe you got eight?

The point here isn't to shame you but to show you that success as the target of life is woefully inadequate. In a recent study, over 60 percent of American adults said they are too busy to enjoy life.[62] Parents, it's worse for you. Seventy-four percent of American parents say they are too busy to enjoy life.

Anxiety is on the rise.

Depression is through the roof.

Suicide rates continue to climb.

There is a problem. In his book on the Sabbath, Wayne Muller observed that a "successful" life has become a violent enterprise. Listen to how he continues:

> We make war on our own bodies, pushing them beyond their limits; war on our children, because we cannot find enough time to be with them when they are hurt and afraid, and need our company; war on

our spirit, because we are too preoccupied to listen to the quiet voices that seek to nourish and refresh us; war on our communities, because we are fearfully protecting what we have, and do not feel safe enough to be kind and generous; war on the earth, because we cannot take the time to place our feet on the ground and allow it to feed us, to taste its blessings and give thanks.[63]

The problem is not success. The problem is not the attainment of wealth, position, honors, or the like. The problem is making success your target.

It's the Sisyphean Effect.

It's the impossible task.

It will impact your health. Even worse, it might kill your soul.

◎ ◎ ◎

"I spent a lot of years aiming at the target of success," Patric says, shaking his head as he sips the final ounce of his flat white. My friend Patric owns a *successful* digital marketing firm.

"I spent a lot of years winning trophies my mom threw in the trash," I say in response.

I used to think, When *I become a professional soccer player,* then *I'll be happy.* I used to think, When *I drive this car,* then *I'll be satisfied.* I used to think, When *I get this degree,* then *I'll be content*. I got those things. I'm glad I did. They were thrilling and exciting; they brought me joy…but then I always wanted something more.

This is the problem of aiming your life at the target of success: the summit never comes; there is no end to the pursuit. There is a better way though. There's a better target. There is a solution:

Aim at *significance*.

I've spent the last twenty years with significance as my goal. I haven't always hit the target, but the shift isn't as difficult as you might think. It involves a new perspective, and a new priority, and a new pursuit, but you can do it. You can access life to the full.

Maybe it seems scary to give up the pursuit of success.

Maybe it feels daunting to shift the aim of your life.

But think about Sisyphus. He pushed the same rock up the same hill…*forever*. I would ask him the same question I'll ask you:

What do you have to lose?

PART TWO:

The Solution

We will not wish we had made more money, acquired more stuff, lived more comfortably, taken more vacations, watched more television, pursued greater retirement, or been more successful in the eyes of this world. Instead, we will wish we had given more of ourselves to living for the day when every nation, tribe, people, and language will bow around the throne and sing the praises of the Savior.

—David Platt

Chapter 4

A NEW PERSPECTIVE

I went for a bike ride the other day. You'd think I'd know where I'm going in my own town. Apparently, I do not.

"Where are we?" I shout.

My cycling partner Bobby says, "I think we're almost home."

We'd been riding for three hours, and I was out of water. It didn't seem like we were *almost home* to me.

"Ride faster," Bobby says. Now waving one hand like an air traffic controller in blue spandex, Bobby shouts, "Stay the course!" So, on we ride. And on. And on. Twenty more miles. Then we turn around.

Here's the point: making success the target of your life is like riding a bike in the wrong direction. It doesn't matter how fast you go; you don't end up where you want to be.

There is a solution though.

Turn around.

◎ ◎ ◎

One of my favorite stories involves a man called "lame" who took up residence at a local pool. Where I grew up, we used that term, but not like Jesus did. Here's the story:

Jesus is cruising around Jerusalem one day when he decides to stop at the pool. I wish I knew the mind of God, but I'm not sure why Jesus stopped. It probably had something to do with the man called lame. Other people like this man hung out at the pool—the blind, the sick, the paralyzed, and…the lame. The man Jesus spoke with had been lame for thirty-eight years.[64]

I always imagine this pool like the bar from *Cheers*. It might not be the coolest place in town, but everyone knows your name. Especially if you've been there thirty-eight years.

"Do you want to get well?"[65]

That's what Jesus asked the man called lame. No small talk. No formalities. No introduction. Jesus just walks up to the guy lying by the pool, and that's what he says. *"Do you want to get well?"*

Has God ever asked you a question like that? If God asked you a question like that, what would you say?

Seems like a no-brainer.

The man starts to shout, "Yes! Yes! Yes! Absolutely, Jesus, *I do*! I want to be healed! I want to be revived! I want to be well!"

But that's not what the lame man says. Actually, his response is kind of…well, here it is:

"Sir," the invalid replied, "I have no one to help me into the pool when the water is stirred. While I am trying to get in, someone else goes down ahead of me."[66]

I told you. *Lame.* Right?

Carpe diem.

Maybe the lame man wasn't a fan of ancient Roman poetry? I'm told the expression actually means *pluck the day.*[67] But this guy doesn't pluck anything. He just sits there at the pool with his friends, making excuses for his situation. I don't know about you, but I do that too. Make excuses. Justify. Rationalize. And I never intend to miss God's best plan for my life, but it's easy to be content. It's easy to think things are good enough. Marriage—good enough. Job—good enough. Relationships—good enough. Bank account—well, it's never good enough. But it's still easy to be content. Especially when success is your goal.

◎ ◎ ◎

"I love to win. I won't apologize." That's what my friend Je'rod says as we're polishing off the hummus. He's much bigger than I am, and he's a Super Bowl champion, so I let him have the last bite.

"I love to win too," I say.

"Well, if you love to win, why is success so bad?" says Je'rod.

This conversation, which literally happened over lunch *today*, reminds me: success isn't bad; it's just a bad target for your life. Let's review:

Success doesn't satisfy.

Success can't fulfill.

Success won't suffice if you want *life to the full*.

Significance is altogether different.

Here's how it's defined—*significance*: the quality of being significant or having a meaning.[68] It's also associated with words like compelling, important, powerful, weight, consequence, and critical. Significance is a noun, but it's so much more. Significance is a perspective. Significance is a pursuit. Significance is a purpose. It's also the secret to the life Jesus offers. Look how leadership guru Ken Blanchard describes it:

> Many people measure their success by wealth, recognition, power, and status. There's nothing wrong with those, but if that's all you're focused on, you're missing the boat…if you focus on significance—using your time and talent to serve others—that's when truly meaningful success can come your way.[69]

I like what Khalil Gibran says, "The significance of a man is not in what he attains, but rather what he longs to attain."[70] Give that thought an extra moment. I'm tempted to write it again. I'll trust you to pause and review. Gibran was a nineteenth-century mystic who dabbled in various world religions, but you don't need to agree with his theology to agree with his point. Here it is: significance is found in your target. I like that because it's not contingent on what you *do*.

Stay-at-home mom with three kids.

Student working two jobs to get through school.

Silicon Valley tech employee.

Significance can be your goal.

Small business owner.

Doctor.

Professional athlete.

Significance can be your goal.

Maybe you're retired. Maybe you're in-between jobs. Maybe you're in the military reading this book on your bunk in the desert. You might be a waitress, or a farmer, an Uber driver, or a *pastor...Significance can be your goal.*

The significance of a man is not in what he attains but rather what he longs to attain. I wrote it again. I couldn't resist. But it's really a matter of perspective.

◎ ◎ ◎

I think that's what's so interesting about the question Jesus asked the man called lame. Scholars say there was a certain emphasis to the question, "Do you want to get well?" It might help to add the word *really*. It's not stated; it's implied.

So, here's the question Jesus asks, with some implied emphasis: Do you *really* want to get well?

Man called lame: "Um, yeah, *but…*" queue lame excuse. I'm an invalid. I'm helpless. I'm a victim of my circumstance. I'm _____. You fill in the blank. Remember, we're good at making excuses too. But Jesus just stares blankly. He says nothing. He just waits. For a better response, I assume. Like he doesn't believe him. Like he's not buying it. Like he refuses to pick up what the lame man has thrown down. It's like my friend's Apple Watch.

Have you had this experience? It's crazy, but it's very possible you have.

Here's the scene: we're hanging out with some friends. In church circles, the gathering is called a *small group* or *life group* or some other creative name for a group that intentionally hangs out together. Our group likes to eat smoked meats. Some enjoy drinking wine, like Jesus. So that's what we're doing as ten of us sit around talking about life.

"I've realized I'm addicted to technology," Joel says.

Most of the heads begin to nod. It's not a counseling session, but I'm sure you can relate. Technology is pervasive. It's not an indictment. It just is.

"I'm on my phone in the gym. I use my phone as my alarm

clock. I text while I drive. I check my email *while…*" Joel hesitates, "in the bathroom."

More head nodding. More "ummmm" noises from the group.

Joel says, "I decided to fast from technology this week, and I discovered I don't need technology as much as I thought." It seemed like a positive revelation. The group reacts like the gallery at an early-round PGA event, light clapping and mild affirmation. But that's when, in the same moment that Joel just says he doesn't need technology, Joel's Apple Watch that's on his wrist *says*…(in a super loud, super sassy voice), "Oh *really*, you don't need technology, Joel?"

Have you seen the clip from the movie *Rudy*, where five-foot-six, one hundred-nothin'-pound Rudy Ruettiger finally gets in the last game of his senior year and sacks the quarterback? And the stadium erupts. And people are losing their minds, going crazy. Well, that's how we react to Joel's watch questioning him by name. We're all yelling. And running. And laughing. And screaming. And Joel is so freaked out that he rips the Apple Watch from his wrist, and he flings it across the room. It might have gone out the window, I don't know. It was nine months ago. But Joel has never worn the watch again.

It was a thing.

On many levels.

It's like Joel's *watch* didn't believe him.

I'm guessing that's why Jesus asked the man called lame, "Do you *really* want to get well?"

◎ ◎ ◎

Here's a question. It might be *the* question. Do you *really* want to live? Does that seem morbid? Sorry. It sounded better in my mind. But it's not intended to be a question of life or death. It's really a question of surviving or thriving—what's your goal?

Maybe you started reading this book because you don't know your goal? Or maybe your target in life is *fuzzy*? Not like a bunny. More like your purpose is unclear.

Maybe you knew your purpose once, but you lost it somewhere between Topeka and Memphis? I'm not sure why you'd drive there, but here's what I know: it's not too late to turn around. If you're heading in the wrong direction, if you're on the wrong track, if you're aimed at the wrong target, it's simple—stop what you are doing and go in a new direction. It's like King Solomon says:

> "The prudent see danger and take refuge, but the simple keep going and pay the penalty."[71]

This idea follows me like one of Pavlov's dogs. It doesn't usually salivate on my shoe; it keeps me up at night though. It's just like when our son was younger and he'd stand by the waterfall in our town. It seems like a fine activity. Looking at a waterfall. But what if he slips on a wet rock? What if he falls over? Toddlers do that for no reason, you know. What if he decides to channel his inner Robert Knievel, also called Evel, and he attempts to jump across the entire river? It *could* happen. But the prudent see danger and take refuge.

I'm not saying you should never let your kids stand by a waterfall. I am saying prudence is essential in life.

So, anyone down for some *prudence*? It can't be a bad thing, right? It might take some humility. It might take some apologies. It might take severing a relationship, or quitting a job, or pursuing a dream, or laying one down—I'm not certain what it will take for you to aim at a new target, but I know it's worth it. That is, if *life to the full* sounds good to you.

You might have noticed this thought from Jesus, which is more like a *promise*, guides my life. You might call it my *life verse*. I have a few of them, actually. But John 10:10 is up there for me. Here's the unedited version:

> "The thief comes only to steal and kill and destroy; I have come that they may have life, and have it to the full." (NIV)

We should talk about *the thief*. Let's start with the *life* Jesus says he came to bring. This life is called *full*; it's called *abundant*; it's called *real*; it's called a *rich and satisfying* life. This is the life Jesus has on offer; it's the life God wants for you. Here's the problem—*the thief*.

I know we don't like to talk about the thief. I don't like to talk about the thief. But this *is* life or death. The Bible calls the thief our enemy. He has other names—Accuser, Liar, Tempter, Evil One, Father of Lies—none of them is complimentary. And the thief has a purpose. Did you notice? *Steal and kill and destroy*. That's it. I'll make it personal—the thief wants *you* to miss your life. This is his goal—to keep *you* from experiencing the life Jesus offers.

If this were a book on spiritual warfare, I'd keep going on this point, but you need to understand you have an enemy who wants to keep you from the life God wants for you. Here's one of his greatest tools, at least in Western civilization: comfort.

Now, who doesn't love a good eighteen hundred thread count luxury sheet? Spa day? Yachting on the French Riviera? These are comforts you may or may not know, but they won't necessarily keep you from the life Jesus offers. Becoming too comfortable will. Here's another way to put it: *content*.

The thief wants you to be content.

The thief wants you to accept less than the life Jesus offers.

This is the problem with success as your goal. We're content to strive for wealth, position, honors, or the like because comfort often follows. So, we measure our life by metrics like *achievement, acquisition, high-rank, high-position, triumph, prosperity, profit* and *a favorable outcome*. And when we get those things, we're content...but we always need more.

Don't you see the trick?

Don't you see the ruse?

The thief wants you to stay on the treadmill, like the hamster that just keeps running. It's the Sisyphean Effect. But as long as you're…*content*…to chase the same things on repeat, the thief has accomplished the goal.

So, are you *content*?

Be honest. It's just you and me here. And I'm not even here, really. So, here's the question *you* need to answer. I'll state it in the first person, because it's your question to answer:

Am I content? (*Remember*, yes or no) _____

Is your bank statement enough? Are your investments enough? Is your degree enough? Is your title enough? Is the championship enough? Is the promotion enough? Is the award enough? Is the recognition enough? Are others' opinions of you enough?

Are you content with the pursuit of success?

I hope the answer is no. I pray the answer is no.[72] The problem is, we live in a success-based culture, so even if there's something more, look around, you'll see that most everyone else is content with less. It's why we need a new perspective. It's why Jesus is unwilling to accept an *excuse* from a man called lame.

◎ ◎ ◎

There is a caveat I should share about the man who sat by the pool for thirty-eight years. You might know it. Do you have a Bible? Do you have a Bible app? If you do, great. If you don't, get one. Regardless, let's do an exercise together.

Go ahead, put this book down. Yes, the book you are reading. If you've made it this far, I'm assuming you'll come back. So, put the book down and find John 5:4 in the Bible. Come on. You won't regret it. Remember, games are fun. So. Ready. Go!

[Music from Jeopardy playing softly for ambiance]

[Don't rush. I'm patient. Ask my wife…I waited thirty-five years to get married.]

Ok. Did you find it—John 5:4?

Maybe I should have told you, it's in the New Testament— back half of the Bible—Matthew, Mark, Luke, John. Can you find it now? I used to hate Sunday School because old Mrs. Waters used to make me read aloud. I had to find the Scripture verse first—I hated that even more.

It's the Sisyphean Effect.

Unless you're Shakespeare or just love Elizabethan English, finding John 5:4 is the impossible task—it's not there.[73] Look it up…if you didn't play the game, that is. John chapter 5, verse 4. It's not in my Bible, but here's what the New King James Version says:

For an angel went down at a certain time into the pool and stirred up the water; then whoever stepped in first, after the stirring of the water, was made well of whatever disease he had.

We could probably debate biblical inerrancy here, but that's not the point. Some scholars question the accuracy of this verse. Others don't. Here's what's important for the discussion we're having: the man called lame believed he could be healed if he jumped into the water first. Myth? Urban legend? Hopeful fable? I might ask God one day. But remember the question Jesus asks the man: "Do you want to get well?" The man responds: "I have no one to help me into the pool when the water is stirred. While I am trying to get in, someone else goes down ahead of me."

I wonder if the man called lame thought Jesus would commiserate? Everyone talks about Jesus' compassion. Maybe the man thought Jesus would feel sorry for the thirty-eight years he spent sitting at the pool? Or maybe he was just making an excuse because he was content?

After thirty-eight years, all his friends were at the pool. He made his money begging at the pool. He was known and accepted at the pool. So, this guy's *life* was at the pool. And it probably wasn't perfect. And it might not have been what he dreamed his life would be. It might not even have been that enjoyable, but it was good enough.

The situation could be better, but—it's good enough.

The relationship could be better, but—it's good enough.

The job could be better, but—it's good enough.

Do you ever think like that?

Pastor David Platt makes a piercing observation in his book *Radical: Taking Back Your Faith from the American Dream*:

> I could not help but think that somewhere along the way we had missed what is radical about our faith and we replaced it with what is comfortable.[74]

Sometimes I wonder if I'm too comfortable to want something more. Sometimes I wonder if I'm like the man sitting by the pool.

Do you *really* want to be well?

Do you *really* want life to the full?

◎ ◎ ◎

I can imagine what the man called lame must have thought when Jesus approached him at the pool.

Jesus who?

He doesn't know me.

He hasn't been here the past thirty-eight years.

But the question is simple: "Do you want to get well?" Jesus says.

If you're aimed at the wrong target, if you're currently off track, if you're heading in the wrong direction for any reason, this is the question God is asking you.

Do you really want to get well?

You know how the man called lame responds. He was content. His life wasn't perfect, but it was good enough. So, he makes an excuse.

The pool was all this man knew. The pool was his social network. The pool was his support group. The pool was his livelihood. The pool was *life* from his perspective, but Jesus offers *more*.

You get to choose.

It's a simple formula really.

Same thing + Same way = Same result, every time.

But what if you do the same thing a different way?

What if you don't have to change what you do, but you just have to change why you do it?

What if the secret to significance is as simple as a new perspective?

That's what I love about the story of the man called lame. After thirty-eight years doing the same thing the same way, believing no one would help, no one *could* help. Jesus approaches the man on a day like any day. Maybe a day just like today? *Do you want to get well?* Jesus says.

Man called lame: "Um, yeah, *but…*" queue lame excuse. But Jesus offers no rebuttal. There's no debate. No discussion. No discourse. Jesus just says, "Get up! Pick up your mat and walk."[75] And that's what happens. Immediately, the man called lame was healed.

It's the power of a new perspective. It's the power of Jesus, really. If you're heading one direction and you realize it's not the direction you need to go—turn around.

How?

The answer is a simple question: What do you long to attain?

Chapter 5

A NEW PURPOSE

God called me on the phone one time. At least, I think it
was God. He told me his name was *Jesús*. He worked for the
US Bureau of Consular Affairs. A few years prior, I heard
from God as well. He didn't call on the phone that time, but
there's something unmistakable when you hear his voice.

"I'll go anywhere, God!"

That's what I said out loud as I lay on my bed in South
Africa. I was *released* from the professional soccer team I
was playing for the day before. There's another word for it
in a more corporate setting—I was *fired*.

I went to South Africa to serve God through soccer. I
believed God *called* me to Africa. I believed it was my purpose. But the door closed. Have you ever had an experience
like that? Have you ever believed you had a purpose that
was no longer possible to pursue? It didn't feel good to me.

"I'll go anywhere, God!"

I just kept saying the same thing over and over. I didn't

want to miss my purpose—*twice*. I didn't want to carve my own path or forge my own way. I decided that I wouldn't move until God tells me where to go. He never did. At least not while I was listening. I went any way.

◎ ◎ ◎

I landed in Singapore on a hot, humid summer night. I don't think there *is* another kind of night in Singapore— it's always hot. I don't like to be hot. Maybe that should have been a sign. Maybe I should have been paying more attention. Maybe I shouldn't have left Africa. But I never heard otherwise. So, I took the best deal I could find. I've noticed that happens when your purpose isn't clear.

The Singaporean Professional Soccer League isn't one of the best in the world, but they pay well. I wish I could say I went for a more altruistic reason, but I was a professional soccer player who rarely got paid. So, this was my moment. At least, that's what I thought.

I took a high-speed train from my downtown apartment to the practice facility. It seemed like a dream. When I was young, I always wanted to practice in a big stadium during the week and play in an even bigger stadium on the weekend. That's how it worked in Singapore. I walked from the train station into the stadium. The grass was cut perfectly. The players had brand-new gear. The coaches were all from Europe. It's what I always wanted.

I stopped just before I stepped onto the field. It felt like the culmination of years of hard work. I'm not sure why God chose that moment to speak to me, but he did. Standing there. On the side of the field. Watching my new team-mates warm-up. I heard God's voice.

You don't have to do this.

That's what God said.

I didn't pay attention.

You don't have to do this, God said again.

I've noticed God doesn't use a microphone, but he does speak. The question is, do you know what God's voice sounds like? I didn't. I don't think I had ever heard God say anything before that moment. But it was definitely God. I know because it wasn't my own thought.

I wanted to be famous.

I wanted to make lots of money.

I wanted to drive a Pontiac Firebird Trans Am. Remember? It had to be a *black* Pontiac Firebird Trans Am, with a robotic artificially intelligent electronic computer module.

That was my goal. Even though I was a Christian. Even though I went to church. Even though I went to Africa, then Asia, to serve God. Success was the target of my life. Of course, I didn't tell people that. I don't think I knew it myself. But I know looking back. That's why God spoke to me.

You don't have to prove yourself anymore.

It wasn't audible. It wasn't loud. It wasn't condemning.

But only God could know, my greatest goal was *approval*. When I was ten years old, my coach told me, "You'll never make it!" I spent the next eleven years working to prove him wrong. I needed to prove myself to the fans. I needed to prove myself to coaches. I needed to prove myself to… *myself*. Maybe you can relate? Standing on the side of the field in Singapore, God spoke a new purpose into my life. It happened as fast as you just read this sentence.

"Thanks for having me, Coach."

That's what I said as I walked onto the field for my first practice in Singapore. I never actually touched the ball. I flew back to Africa that night.

◎ ◎ ◎

Jesus often said, "He who has ears to hear, let him hear!"[76] I always thought this saying was gratuitous until I went to Singapore. I always thought I could pursue God and everything else at the same time. I realize now, God's purpose for my life is much bigger than I imagined. Rick Warren wrote a fairly popular book on *purpose*. Listen to what he says:

> The purpose of your life is far greater than your own personal fulfillment, your peace of mind, or even your happiness. It's far greater than your family, your career, or even your wildest dreams and ambitions. If you want to know why you were placed on this planet, you must begin with God. You were born by his purpose and for his purpose.[77]

Why are you here? Wherever you are. It's one of the most important questions you can answer. It's also the solution to missing your life.

What is your purpose?

Let's do another fill in the blank exercise. Ready?

My purpose in life is: _____

_____

I hope you participated. Even Paul, the apostle, completed this exercise while sitting in a Roman jail cell. Paul was chained to two guards. His daily routine consisted of a light morning beating; mocking, ridicule, and demoralization in the afternoon; and, of course, several lashes with cat-o'-nine tails each night. The guards affectionately called it *the cat*—it was their favorite form of torture. The situation seems less than ideal, but here's what Paul writes from prison: "For to me, to live is Christ and to die is gain."[78]

Say what you will, but Paul knew his purpose. Paul believed in his purpose. Paul was committed to his purpose. Are you? Or maybe you just talk a good game? I think that was my problem when I arrived in Singapore.

If Paul wasn't so busy being tortured, or writing large parts of the New Testament, he might have written a book like this one. At least, I'd like to think so. If he did, I think Paul would have presented the question of *purpose* like this:

For me to live is: _____

Let me throw out a few suggestions that might

apply—money, family, friends, fame, career, hobbies, acceptance, approval, a vacation in the Bahamas? What is it for you? What is your *purpose*? This question is critical because how you fill in the blank will determine your focus. And your focus will determine your target. And your target will determine your significance. And your significance…it will determine your fullness of life.

But here's a challenge: most Americans prioritize happiness over everything else.

According to a recent survey, the majority of Americans, 69 percent, say they find their greatest happiness (and meaning) through family. Thirty-four percent of Americans say they find their greatest happiness (and meaning) through career. Twenty-three percent cite money. Nineteen percent cite things like faith, friends, and hobbies. Health also makes the list, as 16 percent of Americans say that good health is an important part of the happiness (and meaning) they find in life.[79]

So, statistically, *you* want to be happy. I get it. I feel the same. I want to be happy. I want my family to be happy. I want to have a meaningful career, make money, have friends, enjoy hobbies…I want it all…in *abundance*. It's why I'm so consumed by the offer Jesus makes: "I have come that they may have life, and have it to the full."[80]

Life to the full.

It's why Jesus came to earth. It's why Jesus died. Have you ever thought about this?

Jesus' *purpose* was to offer life to all who would receive it. Jesus called himself the bread of life.[81] Jesus called himself "the way, the truth, and the life."[82] Speaking to a woman about her dead brother, Jesus shortened his title. Here's what he says: I am…*life*.[83] It's why Jesus came. It's why Jesus died. To offer life. But maybe we confuse happiness with life sometimes? Maybe we think happiness *is* life? Maybe we make happiness our target?

I'll say it straight: happiness is good, but it's a bad target for life.

Happiness is fickle.

Happiness fluctuates.

Happiness is found in what's *happening* around you.

It's the problem of making happiness the goal: *happiness depends on happenings*.

C. S. Lewis once said something about this. He said, "Don't let your happiness depend on something you may lose."[84]

You win the lottery—you're happy. The dog dies—you're not. You get a promotion—happy. Untimely diagnosis—you're not. You're recognized at work—happy. Your kid flunks out of school—you guessed it; happy you are not. But Jesus came and died to offer *a new purpose*, one that yields fixed results.

◎ ◎ ◎

Have you read the *Westminster Shorter Catechism* lately? If you're Presbyterian, maybe? If you're Anglican, there's an even better chance. But 375 years after its publication, some of us have missed something important found in these 107 questions. Here's question number one:

What is the chief end of man?[85]

It's really the question of purpose. It just sounds better.

Russian novelist Fyodor Dostoyevsky addressed the question of purpose in his book *The Brothers Karamazov*. It's 880 pages long, so I'll just tell you what he says: The mystery of human existence lies not in just staying alive, but in finding something to live for.

Dostoyevsky's characters believed that without a concrete idea of what he was living for, man would refuse to live. It feels *extreme* to me. But here's a small portion of the full dialogue between Dostoyevsky's imaginative character, The Grand Inquisitor of the Spanish Inquisition, and this Jesus-like figure:

> Without a stable conception of the object of life, man would not consent to go on living, and would rather destroy himself than remain on earth, though he had bread in abundance. That is true. But what happened? Instead of taking men's freedom from them, Thou didst make it greater than ever! Didst Thou forget that man prefers peace, and even death, to freedom of choice in the knowledge of good and evil?[86]

Author, psychologist, and Holocaust survivor Victor Frankl put it like this, "Those who have a 'why' to live, can bear with almost any 'how.'"[87]

It's the question of purpose.

It's the chief end of man.

Here's how the *Westminster Shorter Catechism* answered the question in 1676: What is the chief end of man?

To glorify God, and to enjoy him forever.

It's *why* you are here.

God once spoke to a guy named Simon about his purpose. Jesus called him Peter. Actually, Jesus didn't just speak to Peter, he got in Peter's boat. Peter was a fisherman. Peter's father was a fisherman. I'm guessing his father's father and his father's father's father were fishermen too. Here's the point: Peter understood how to fish. Jesus did not. But he still got into Peter's boat to begin a conversation.

Has God ever spoken to you?

You would need to you know what God's voice sounds like, but if you do, what did God say?

"Put out into deep water, and let down the nets for a catch."[88]

That's what God said to Peter, the fisherman.

How would you respond?

"Yes! I'll do it! Whatever you say, Jesus! You're God. I'm not. I'll follow your lead."

That's what I would say if God offered me fishing advice. But I'm not a fisherman. My father likes to fish, but it's not his profession. And my father's father never went fishing at all. So, maybe it's easy to follow Jesus when you don't feel like you know what to do. But what if God tells you to do something that seems contradictory to what you've been taught or what you've experienced or what's created *success* in your life before?

That's probably why Peter says: "Master, we've worked hard all night and haven't caught anything."[89]

Can you blame Peter for his response? He was up all night. Working hard. Plying his trade. Then Jesus comes along peddling free advice. Jesus is God, but still…he's not a fisherman. So, Peter makes an *excuse*. I probably would have been more direct if Jesus approached me on the soccer field and offered a lesson in taking penalty kicks. "I'm the expert, Jesus." That's what I would say. "Leave it with me."

Do you ever think like that? Do you ever find yourself thinking you know better than God? It's not advisable, but I do. It's not my goal. It's not even my desire, but inadvertently, I do it all the time. It's like the man called lame who sat by the pool for thirty-eight years. Jesus asked him a simple question, "Do you want to be well?"[90]

"Um, yeah, *but…*"

Just like Peter, the man called lame made an *excuse*. The

irony is that he wanted to be well. Purpose works the same way. You are free to choose what you live for—happiness, health, family, friends, hobbies…you get to choose. What's your goal? What's your target? What is your *purpose*?

You can choose anything you want, but if you want life to the full, choose significance—and not your own—the *significance* of God.

◎ ◎ ◎

Remember, *significance*: "the quality of being significant or having a meaning."[91] It's also defined by words like *compelling, important, powerful, weight, consequence,* and *critical.*

It seems significance is very…*significant* in the Bible. In the Old Testament it's synonymous with *glory*; it's the Hebrew word *kavod.* Here's what it means: "weight as measured on a scale."[92] It's our purpose. Jesus says it's why we're here.

Weight as measured on a scale.

Is this *your* goal?

When you brush your teeth. When you style your hair. When you drive your car or go to work or kiss your wife… Paul says: "So, whether you eat or drink or whatever you do, do it all for the glory of God."[93]

I used to write that Scripture verse on my cleats when I played soccer. Sometimes I'd write in Latin—*Soli Deo Gloria*—it means the same thing. I stole the idea from the seventeenth-century composer Johann Sebastian Bach.

He would never sign his name on any musical score, he'd simply write the initials *S. D. G.* in the bottom right corner when he was satisfied with his work.

S. D. G.

I started writing it on my cleats long before I lived it as my purpose.

I wonder if you ever do that? Do you ever know the right thing to do, but you still do something different? It seems to work like that with significance. Maybe that's why this fan in California used to always ask players the same question?

"*To who?*"

That's what he would shout anytime you made a bad pass.

"*To who?*"

He'd yell, with his meaty hands cupped around his enormous mouth. He sat in the very middle of the stadium. He always wore the same hat. It was a sombrero to be exact. *To who are you passing? To who are you shooting?* It really was annoying because the question isn't grammatically correct. But it didn't stop this fan from asking the question on repeat.[94]

I wonder if it's the question God might ask us about our purpose?

Think about it. God has given you time, talents, resources, and degrees; God has provided family, friends, jobs, houses, cars, and everything else you have. But God also gives you a choice. You get to choose your purpose.

So, maybe God is sitting on the sideline of your life, wearing a sombrero, shouting, "*To who*?"

I can't imagine God would use improper grammar, but I'm sure he wants to know: *To whom is your life lived*? It's an important question regardless of God's choice of hats.

Do you live for the significance of God or the significance of yourself?

Do you work to reveal the weight of God's glory or your own?

Do you eat or drink or drive your car or post on social media to make much of God, or are you more concerned about making much of who you are?

It's the question of purpose.

It's the chief end of man.

To glorify God or…well, you get to choose.

◎ ◎ ◎

Paul says there's a day coming when the choice of significance will be chosen for you:

> At the name of Jesus every knee should bow, in heaven and on earth and under the earth, and every tongue confess that Jesus Christ is Lord, to the glory of God the Father.[95]

It's our purpose: the glory of God the Father.

It's why I'm here.

It's why you're here.

It's why God spoke to me. Standing on the side of a field in Singapore. Watching my new teammates warm-up.

You don't have to do this, God says.

I'll just do it for one season, I think.

You don't have to do this, God says.

I'll just make enough money to fund all the good work I want to do for you *in the future*. That's what I say to God.

You don't have to do this, God says.

There's nothing wrong with playing soccer in Singapore! I was sure that would stump him.

Here's what God said to me: *You choose.*

So, compare the options—my glory versus God's?

What is your purpose?

Honestly, I don't think it's a difficult choice. Especially if you're looking for a fixed result.

Chapter 6

A NEW PURSUIT

Imagine you are dead. Seriously. Maybe you were one hundred? Maybe you were one hundred and two? Choose whatever age you want for this exercise, but imagine you are dead.

It's the day of your funeral. Different people start to arrive. Can you see who's there? Your family? Friends? Neighbors? Colleagues? Followers on Instagram? How many people attend?

Your funeral begins. What's the mood? Are people sad? Happy? Joyous? Grateful? Regretful? What's the vibe?

My friend once told me he doesn't care what happens at his funeral as long as they play *My Way* by Frank Sinatra. It's a good thought. But I think he would care, if he could.

It's your funeral. Listen carefully. What do people say? What did people most appreciate about you? What did your life mean to them? What impact did you have? What kind of person were you to those who are there?

It's your funeral. There's one caveat: you can't change anything when you're dead. Here's the good news: you aren't dead yet.[96]

◎ ◎ ◎

If you could only choose one word to describe the life of Mother Teresa, which would you choose:

Success or significance?

Circle your choice.

Her given name was Anjezë Gonxhe Bojaxhiu. "Mother Teresa" definitely rolls off the tongue more easily! Born in 1910 in Skopje, the capital of The Republic of Macedonia, young Anjezë left home at eighteen to become a Catholic nun in Ireland. Within months, she was given permission to travel to India, where she would live and work the rest of her life.

Not all of us can do great things. But we can "do small things with great love."[97]

That was Mother Teresa's mantra; it was also her calling card. She wasn't impressive in stature, education, or wealth. But her life had *impact*.

In 1950 Mother Teresa founded The Missionaries of Charity. Here's how she described the mission: to care for "the hungry, the naked, the homeless, the crippled, the blind, the lepers, all those people who feel unwanted, unloved, uncared for throughout society, people that have become a burden to the society and are shunned by everyone."[98] She would later add other groups: refugees, former prostitutes, the mentally ill, abandoned children, people with AIDS, the aged, and the convalescent.[99] I think that covers everyone. Everyone that no one else will care for, that is.

Mother Teresa lived in the slums of Calcutta for over fifty years.

Mother Teresa served the poor and destitute.

Mother Teresa had three material possessions when she died: a bucket and two saris.[100]

A few years ago, I visited a home for terminally ill women in Calcutta. Mother Teresa founded the home, but she wasn't there. By Western standards, the home was… *rough*…at best. There were exposed power sources and leaking ceilings. I left my shoes at the front door when I entered, and when I left, a large cockroach had claimed them as its own. I'm guessing you wouldn't want to live there. You might not even want to visit there. But there was something that stood out. Not just the smell; it was *significant*. But here's what you notice at Mother Teresa's home for terminally ill women: joy. It's everywhere.

The women in Mother Teresa's home are terminally ill. They all know they will die—soon. They know their days are numbered and their situation is less than ideal. But I noticed that they all celebrate the life they have. It made me wonder if I *live* like that. Do I celebrate each day as a gift from God? Do I approach each day as a problem or a prize?

A few days later I visited another home for mentally and physically impaired children. I was told most of them were abandoned at birth because of their abnormalities. Mother Teresa founded this home too. It was similar to the home for the terminally ill women though it was located in New Delhi and the living conditions were noticeably *worse*. There was still the undeniable presence of *joy*. There was still the same sense of the celebration of life.

Have you ever been confronted by abject poverty? What about extreme social circumstances? This is the pursuit to which Mother Teresa gave her life, not fame, not fortune, not comfort or convenience. For over fifty years Mother Teresa spent her life in relative obscurity, living among people few others would think to serve, but when she died, over fifteen thousand people gathered at Netaji Indoor Stadium in Calcutta, and thousands more lined the streets to pay their respects as her body was carried by.

President K. R. Narayanan and Prime Minister I. K. Gujral of India were there. Jordan's Queen Noor, and Spain's Queen Sofia were there. The presidents of Italy, France, and the Philippines were there. Even Hilary Clinton, then first lady of the United States, was there.[101] At the funeral of a woman who spent her entire life serving the poor.

Success or significance.

What do you think Saint Teresa of Calcutta pursued?

Here's a more important question: What do you pursue?

◎ ◎ ◎

I had a professor in college my freshman year who reminded me of Mother Teresa. Well, he wasn't Catholic, kind, or concerned for others, but he was really short. He also had an accent. Like my ninety-nine-year-old Japanese grandmother. And I should have mentioned this—Mr. Miyagi was one of my grandmother's best friends. Really. His name was Pat Morita. He was hilarious from what I recall. It's probably why I liked this professor, even though he was a scary little man.

To protect the innocent, I'll omit this professor's name, though I believe there's now a hotline for students who've been whacked in the head by teachers with rulers, erasers, or colored pens of any sort. Let's just say, Professor X didn't mess around. *So,* it's the last day of class before the semester final, and Professor X has just reviewed the content for the test. I am sitting with many of the other athletes in the very back row of this enormous lecture hall.

"Any question!"

That's what Professor X says. It was more of a statement than a question. Even now, over twenty years later, I'm certain he wasn't looking for a response.

The class is silent.

No one talks. No one moves. Professor X scans the room looking for his next victim. It seems we've made it through the class relatively unscathed, *until*…front-row-sitter raises his hand.

Nooo! I think to myself. I'm certain there was a collective *Nooooooo* in the mind of *everyone* in the room. He did it anyway. He raised his hand. He asked the question. He poked the bear. It doesn't matter what the question was, Professor X clearly wasn't happy.

Have you ever seen a Shar Pei puppy? That's what Professor X's face looked like as he considered his response. And there was the squeal. Maybe it was more of a whistle, or it could have been a whining noise? Whatever it was, it was definitely scary. It sounded like…

"Eeeeeeeeewwwwww!"

The noise went on for, what seemed to be, minutes. Professor X's face was still in full Shar Pei puppy mode. Now standing over said front-row-sitter, Professor X pulls out an old school extendable pointer. And the noise intensifies.

"Eeeeeeeeewwwwww…" he says. "You are dumb student!" *Pause for dramatic effect.*

Queue whacking.

"I tell you all the answer. Now you ask dumb question!"

I'm sure that's what Professor X said as he hit poor front-row-sitter with his extendable pointer. It's hard to be sure with his accent. But I never saw front-row-sitter again.

I wonder sometimes if God is like Professor X. Not necessarily short, Asian, or mean, but maybe God is tempted to think something similar of us?

Dumb student.

Not you, of course. Everyone else. All of us who seek God, who want God's best, who read God's Word, and want God's heart. But we still go our own way. We do our own thing. We follow our neighbor more than we follow God.

It's frustrating to God, I'm sure. It's not a new condition though. The Israelites acted the same way as they set up life in the promised land. Here's what the prophet Samuel observed, "In those days Israel had no king; all the people did whatever seemed right in their own eyes."[102]

Right in their own eyes.

I've realized, this is my problem. Maybe it's your problem too? God has clearly told us how we should live; he's told us our purpose—to glorify him. He's given us his Spirit as our guide. Jesus tells us he wants us to experience *life to the full*. It's why he came. It's why he died. It's what God wants for us. But what do we do? We pursue things of this world more than we pursue God.

Why is this happening?

Why is this like this?

Why do I feel like I do?

Do you ever ask God questions like this? Do you ever wonder *why* you don't feel satisfied? *Why* whatever you do is never enough? *Why* abundant life eludes you?

"I tell you all the answer. Now you ask dumb question!"

Maybe that's what God would say to us. With all love. With all compassion. With all the empathy possible. Maybe God thinks we're dumb sometimes. And we tell our five-year-old son not to say *dumb*, but it's like they say, *if the shoe fits*…even if there's a cockroach now living inside.

So, maybe we need to answer the question:

Is there anything more important than pursuing God?

◎ ◎ ◎

The disciples wrestled with the same questions we do. Think about Peter, the fisherman. One day he's out living his everyday, ordinary life, fishing on the Sea of Galilee, when Jesus calls to him: "Follow me."[103] It's the same invitation Jesus gave to other disciples like Andrew, James, and John.

Follow me.

It's an invitation. It's also the pursuit that leads to *life to the full*.

Here's the challenge: there are many good things to follow. Let's name a few:

Doctor

Accountant

Lawyer

Teacher

Coach

Counselor

Pastor

What about the news? What about social media? What about your friends? The question is, what or *whom* do you follow most? It's an important question, even for guys like Peter, the fisherman. When Jesus said *follow me,* that's what Peter did. For three years, Peter followed Jesus everywhere. Peter was there when Jesus walked on water. Peter was there when Jesus brought a dead girl back to life. Peter was at the last supper, in the garden of Gethsemane; he witnessed the crucifixion. Peter *followed* Jesus. That is, until he didn't.

The word *follow* means *pursue* in the original language. It's to proceed after, to chase, or to diligently seek. It's what Peter did, he *pursued* Jesus. That is, until he didn't.

I don't know if you've noticed this, but there's a story told in the Gospel of John that occurs after Jesus' death. It involves Peter and some other disciples. Here's what it says:

> Jesus appeared again to his disciples, by the Sea of Galilee. It happened this way: Simon Peter, Thomas... Nathanael...the sons of Zebedee, and two other disciples were together. "I'm going out to fish," Simon Peter told them, and they said, "We'll go with you." So they went out and got into the boat, but that night they caught nothing.[104]

Does this story sound familiar to you? Maybe you've read it? Maybe you heard a sermon about it? Or maybe you recognize it because it's the *exact same scenario* in which Peter first met Jesus? Here's the difference: it's three years later, and Jesus was crucified, and Peter saw Jesus hang on the cross, and Peter watched Jesus die, *so*…Peter thinks Jesus is dead.

It makes sense, right?

There is one small nuance to the story though. Did you notice where Peter goes when he thinks Jesus is dead? Yup—right back to his old life—to his old friends, his old job, to his old daily routine. Even though Jesus told the disciples he would go to the cross. Even though Jesus told them he would be crucified. Even though Jesus told *everyone* he would rise from the grave on the third day. Peter still went back to his old life. So, here's the question:

Was Peter pursuing Jesus or something else?

I recently went out to dinner with my wife at one of our favorite spots. We were in Cleveland, and it was winter, so of course, it was snowing outside. Crazy. I know.

My wife is always stunning, but she looked extra stunning this particular night. So, after dinner, I remember the chivalry lesson I took in sixth grade, and I decide to pull the car up so my wife won't have to walk through the snow.

Now while I was sitting in my car waiting by the curb just across the street from the restaurant, I notice this guy pointing in my direction. I don't know him. I don't think I've ever seen him. But what do you do when someone points at you? I wave. I smile. The guy is still pointing at me, so I give him a quick thumbs up.

I thought the interaction was over, but now this guy is walking toward my car.

Wait. What. Who is this guy?

That's what I'm thinking as he's walking across the street. I lock my doors. I make my best angry face. I brace myself as he starts knocking on my window.

"Let me in!" the guy yells.

"What? I can't hear you," I say. Of course, I could hear him; I just couldn't think of anything better to say.

"Let me in!" he yells again.

I had *no idea* what was happening. Was this guy trying to hijack my car? Was he trying to rob me? Was he part of a terrorist organization looking to abduct middle-aged half-Japanese retired athletes? I couldn't know. But there was *no* chance I was opening the door.

The man moves from knocking to pounding on my window. I keep thinking, *Where is my wife*? But she never arrives. So, it's a stand-off. This guy clearly won't leave. I won't open the door. So, I decide to roll down my window…three inches.

"What do you want?" I yell through the very small crack that separates us. Still making my best angry face. Still lacking substantial intimidation of any kind.

"I want to get in the car," he says.

"*Why*?" I yell.

"Dude, you're my Uber driver, right?" he says.

My fear immediately dissipates. My ineffective angry face turns to a smile. I roll my window down a few more inches, and say, "Nope. I'm just a guy, sitting in his car, waiting for his wife."

Have you noticed, it's not always obvious what you should do in life? It's true when strange men knock on your car window. It's true when unexpected things happen or scenarios arise that you couldn't predict. It's also true when you consider what you should pursue most.

Money.

Sex.

Notability.

Approval.

There are many things you can chase. There are many things you can diligently seek after in life. But here's the question: How do you want to be remembered? What impact do you want your life to have on the world? And just as important, do you really want *life to the full*?

I appreciate how C. S. Lewis frames it:

> Aim at Heaven and you will get Earth "thrown in": aim at Earth and you will get neither.[105]

Jesus says something similar when he compares the sum of our life to *treasure*. It's our choice—we get to choose how we spend our life. Here's how Jesus says it:

> Don't store up treasures here on earth, where moths eat them and rust destroys them, and where thieves break in and steal. Store your treasures in heaven, where moths and rust cannot destroy, and thieves do not break in and steal. Wherever your treasure is, there the desires of your heart will also be.[106]

I don't know if Jesus ever did archery in high school, but I'm pretty sure he's saying that whatever you aim at, whatever you most pursue, that's where the majority of your attention, affection, and effort will be. So, this is important: What or *whom* do you choose to follow? Because, whatever or whomever it is, you'll inevitably organize and prioritize your life around that pursuit.

Wherever your treasure is, there the desires of your heart will also be.

◎ ◎ ◎

Maybe I'm weird but I often think about heaven. I like to think about the first thing I'll say to God when I'm standing in his presence. *Why did bad things happen to good people? How does the Trinity work, exactly? How did* Survivor *make it for over forty seasons?* I also like to think about what God will say to me.

"Well done, good and faithful servant!"

It's what Jesus says we should seek to hear from God.

Have you ever noticed, Jesus doesn't say we should aspire to hear God say, "Well done, good and *successful* servant!" There's no mention of a *good and famous* servant or a *good and wealthy* servant. Jesus doesn't say we should seek to hear the words "*good and powerful* servant" either.

There's something very good about being faithful.

I don't know if faithful is your stated life goal, but research suggests the majority of us want to be remembered for the value we have added to other people, specifically our family. One study reveals more than two-thirds (69 percent) of Americans say they most want to be remembered for the memories they shared with those they loved most.[107] People often reference values they pass to their kids as being most important. People talk about life lessons they were able to share. People often say relationships are what they want to be remembered for.

It makes me wonder, will anyone arrive in heaven and say to God, "I wish I had kept my house cleaner!" Maybe people will stand at the pearly gates and say, *I wish I had worried more about what others thought of me.* Or *I wish I had mowed my lawn more.* Or *I wish I had a more prestigious title.* Or *I wish I had been more consumed by my job.* Maybe people will say things like this to God. Maybe. But I don't think so.

Bronnie Ware has written a compelling book based on her time caring for terminally ill patients in their last twelve weeks of life. In *The Top Five Regrets of The Dying*, Ware shares these regrets:

1. I wish I'd had the courage to live a life true to myself, not the life others expected of me.

2. I wish I hadn't worked so hard.

3. I wish I'd had the courage to express my feelings.

4. I wish I had stayed in touch with my friends.

5. I wish that I had let myself be happier.[108]

Of course, this is only one woman's experience interacting with several hundred dying people in Australia, but it seems significant that no one mentions a lack of *success* as their regret. Very few people arrive at the end of their life and wish they had made more money. Almost no one reflects on life and thinks they should have driven a nicer car. Here's how Mother Teresa put it:

> "God has not called me to be successful; He has called me to be faithful."[109]

It's a totally countercultural ambition.

It's altogether different than what most people pursue.

Success or significance—you get to choose.

Mother Teresa chose significance; it worked out pretty well for her.

Peter, the fisherman had a little *wobble* when Jesus died,

but he ultimately chose significance too. Here's what Jesus says about Peter: "You are Peter, and on this rock I will build my church,"[110] and *the entire world* is different because Peter was faithful to God.

That's what I want. That's my goal. This has become the target of my life: significance.

It's what Jesus invites us to pursue.

Follow me, Jesus says.

It's an invitation to proceed after or in a like direction, to chase, and to diligently seek God…more than everything else.

It's an invitation to be faithful.

It might not be the most popular pursuit, but maybe you're like me, just a little. Maybe you're tired of pursuing things that don't satisfy. Maybe you're bored chasing things that can't fulfill. Maybe you don't want to miss your life.

Here's the good news: you aren't dead yet.

So, choose.

INTERMISSION

INTERMISSION

The *Why* Is Your Way

Let's *pause.*

If you're anything like me, the idea of slowing down seems like a waste of time. Delay? Postpone? Wait? I've never been a fan. There are things to do. Tasks to check off the list. If I were reading this book, I'd probably be listening to it on an audio download playing at least one and a half times the normal speed. But there is something to be said for intermission.

As an athlete, I always welcomed halftime. If we were winning, it was an opportunity to refocus. If we were losing, it was a chance to regroup.

I don't know how you feel—are you winning or losing in life? Is your marriage everything you want it to be? How's your relationship with your kids? Career heading in the right direction? How's your soul?

Here's some good news: intermission is an opportunity to refocus and regroup.

Selah is the term the psalmists used. It's a mysterious word, but I've always thought of it as an invitation from God to reflect. So, here's your invitation. Let's *reflect...*

Success doesn't satisfy.

Success can't fulfill.

Success won't suffice if you want life to the full.

Significance is altogether different.

Selah.

We're going to discuss three practical ways to pursue significance in the next section, but let's make sure we agree on *why*. Have you heard of Shahab-ud-din Muhammad Khurram? Come on...the seventeenth-century Mughal emperor? Remarkable military leader? Wealthy? Handsome? Lots of wives? Ring a bell? His friends called him Shah Jahan.

It's said Shah Jahan was the most influential Mughal leader of all time.

Born on January 5, 1592, in Lahore, modern-day Pakistan, Shah was the third son of Prince Salim. Do a quick search on his curriculum vitae—it's impressive. The guy was a builder—armies, cities, the Mughal Empire—Shah built stuff. But there's one thing he built that stands out.

The Taj Mahal.

It was Shah Jahan's life work. It's called one of the Seven Wonders of the World. It cost about one billion dollars in today's currency, and it took over twenty years to build. Here's the question: Do you know *why* Shah Jahan commissioned the Taj Mahal? I'll give you a hint. Her name is…

Mumtaz Mahal.

Apparently, Mumtaz was Shah's favorite wife, but she died prematurely while giving birth to their…*brace yourself*… fourteenth child. It's why Shah commissioned what is today the most famous mausoleum in the world. Or is it a mausoleum?

By definition, a mausoleum is a building constructed to house a tomb. And that was Shah's intent when Mumtaz died in 1632. Shah and his crew immediately began construction, literally, right over the wooden box that housed Mumtaz' remains. And they built around the wooden box for many years. And the more they built, the more passionate about the mausoleum Shah Jahan became. Here's the problem: at a certain point, Shah Jahan had become so passionate about the *building* of the Taj Mahal that he failed to notice when some of the builders, who kept tripping over the annoying wooden box in the middle of their building site, decided to throw the wooden box in the garbage.

One of the most impressive architectural achievements in the world—yes. One of the greatest tributes to a tragedy of life—yes. One of the Seven Wonders of the World—yes. A mausoleum—no. Not if Mumtaz is in the garbage.

◎ ◎ ◎

There is an important lesson to learn from Shah Jahan:

When you lose your *why*, you lose your way.

I'm not talking about misplacing your keys. Or forgetting where you left your cell phone. I'm talking about purpose. It's your *why*. It's your reason for doing what you do. It's the reason you get out of bed each day. It's your goal.

Do you know why you do what you do?

Shah Jahan began with a very clear why. His purpose was to build a mausoleum for the remains of his favorite wife. His objective was to honor her memory, to memorialize her passing. And he was committed to that goal. And he worked for years pursuing that purpose. But somewhere along the way, Shah Jahan started focusing on other things.

Does that ever happen to you? When life gets busy? When you're living in the margins? When you find yourself going through the motions of everyday life? Do you ever forget *why* you do what you?

Do you ever focus on the task more than the goal?

Change the diaper. Mow the lawn. Make the food. Sweep the floor. These are domestic. There are other tasks. Close the deal. Finish the project. Get the grade. Win the game. The list goes on. The tasks of life never end. But there's a difference between a task and a goal. There's a difference between doing something and the reason why you do it. At least, there should be.

It's easy to confuse a task and a goal. Especially when you're right in the middle of all the stuff of life. So, let me say it slightly different:

The why is your way.

If you want life to the full.

The why is your way. If you want life that is truly life.

The why is your way. If you want the best of what God wants for you.

The why is your way.

Here's the problem: it's easy to lose your why. Maybe you've experienced this. Maybe it's why you started reading this book. I don't know why you do what you do, but if you want life to the full, here's what I know: you must know your why.

◎ ◎ ◎

There was a prophet in the Old Testament who compared our lives to grass. I didn't appreciate the idea at first, but think about it:

> All people are like grass, and all their faithfulness is like the flowers of the field. The grass withers and the flowers fall, because the breath of the LORD blows on them. Surely the people are grass.[111]

The psalmist says something similar. It's more direct, I think:

> As for man, his days are like grass; he flourishes like a flower of the field; for the wind passes over it and it is gone.[112]

When our son was born, people kept telling my wife and me, "The days are long, but the years are short." It felt... *unhelpful*, at the time. But here's what you learn: life is brief. So, here's the question, again:

Why do you do what you do?

Why do you work?

Why do you vacation?

Why do you spend time with your kids?

Why do you read?

Why do you pray?

Why do you go to church?

Maybe these are simple questions. Maybe not. Maybe you wake up each day and live on purpose. Honestly, that's the goal. It's *my* goal: to live on purpose, to pursue life to the full. It's why I decided to aim at significance instead of success.

Why do you do what you do?

It's important to know the answer. It's important you don't forget.

Remember, there's a difference between a task and a goal, between knowing what to do and why you do it.

I think every seventeenth-century Mughal emperor would agree: the why is your way.

Selah.

PART THREE:

Three Practical Ways to Pursue Significance

Our greatest fear in life should not be of failure, but of succeeding at something that doesn't really matter.

—D. L. Moody

Chapter 7

BECOME RICH TOWARD GOD

"The Merchant of Death is Dead!"

That was the headline of a French newspaper in 1888. The article described a cold, aloof, uncaring man who had amassed great wealth helping people kill each other through his life's work, the invention of dynamite.

He died.

A Swedish chemist named Alfred read the article. His brother Ludvig had died the same week in France. When Alfred finished reading the article, he threw the newspaper to the ground and covered his face with his hands; he was completely distraught with grief.

How could they think such horrible things? How could they believe I am such a tyrant? Am I really such a bad person?

These thoughts raced through Alfred's head as he sat with his hands over his face. Apparently, the editor of the French newspaper had inadvertently confused Alfred for his brother Ludvig, so instead of reading his brother's obituary, Alfred, who was still living, read his own.

As the story goes, Alfred made a decision that day; he resolved to use his wealth to change his legacy. Eight years later, when Alfred died, he left the equivalent of $244 million to fund an award for people whose work would benefit humanity. You might not have heard of Alfred Nobel, but I'm guessing you've heard of his award. There are actually five awards housed under one name:

The Nobel Prize.

I'm almost certain Alfred Nobel would tell you that no one ever drifts to significance. It's not like significance is a remote-controlled car left in the hall by your five-year-old son. And when you walk in the house carrying all the groceries, you trip, fall, break the eggs, bruise your elbow (and your ego), and your wife laughs and says you're clumsy. Not that that happened to me, of course. But here's the point: you never fall into significance. You don't glide to significance either.

You *choose* significance.

You choose your target.

You choose your goal.

That's what I love about Alfred Nobel. He's not remembered as *The Merchant of Death*. And I've never heard anyone talk about this global ambassador for peace as cold, aloof, or uncaring because, at a certain point, Alfred Nobel made a choice; he decided to invest his life in something with lasting value.

Here's the reality: we don't all have $244 million dollars to fund an award for people whose work will benefit humanity. But we can all choose significance…and life to the full. It begins with God. Consider Blue Zones.

Blue Zones are regions of the world where people live much longer than everyone else. The term made its debut in 2005 when Dan Buettner wrote a cover story in the National Geographic magazine. He called it "The Secrets of a Long Life." Now, just because you live longer than other people, it doesn't mean your goal is significance, but there's an interesting parallel when you look at the common characteristics of people from these zones. Here's what Buettner says:

> Scientific studies suggest that only about 25 percent of how long we live is dictated by genes…The other 75 percent is determined by our lifestyles and the everyday choices we make.[113]

There are nine evidence-based common denominators among people who live in Blue Zones, particularly centenarians, people who live one hundred years or more. Buettner lists these factors in no particular order, but it's interesting that of the 263 centenarians interviewed across the world, 258 have a strong commitment to a faith-based community and attend a faith-based service at least four times per month.[114] Apparently, God adds four to fourteen years to your life; look at the research.[115]

Again, just because you live longer than other people, it doesn't mean you experience life to the full or significance, but maybe we should ask people from Okinawa, Sardinia, Nicoya, Icaria, or the Seventh-day Adventists in Loma Linda, California, what they think. I'm guessing they'd agree with my favorite fourth-century theologian, Augustine of Hippo. His friends call him *Saint* Augustine. Here's what he says: "Thou madest us for Thyself, and our heart is restless, until it repose in Thee."[116]

Rick Warren says something similar to Saint Augustine, just modernized: "Without God, life has no purpose, and without purpose, life has no meaning. Without meaning, life has no significance or hope."[117]

Without God, life has no significance.

It's scientific. It's evidence based. It's the *Blue Zone* discovery.

Without God, you have less life.

◎ ◎ ◎

Maybe it's too simple, but if you really want life to the full, start here: organize your life around the things of God. Here's another way to say it: if you want to pursue significance, pursue God.

Jesus says it like this: "Seek first the kingdom of God and his righteousness, and all these things will be added to you."[118] I love how Eugene Peterson interprets this idea. Here's how he puts it in The Message translation of the Bible:

> Steep your life in God-reality, God-initiative, God-provisions. Don't worry about missing out. You'll find all your everyday human concerns will be met.[119]

Steep your life in God.

It's such a strong visual. It makes me think of taking my son to get ice cream.

"I'll have milkiest chocolate with rainbow sprinkles, please!" he says to the teenage girl behind the counter. He orders the same thing every time.

"How many sprinkles do you want?" says the girl, now pouring the tiny rainbow pellets into my son's bowl.

"A little more," he says, standing on his tiptoes peering over the counter. "Even more," he says, with a huge smile on his face. "Keep going…*more, more, more*," he shouts… until sprinkles are overflowing onto the floor.

Of course, he goes right to sleep after all the ice cream and sprinkles. Or not. But here's the point: life to the full happens when you *overflow* with God.

I'm convinced this is the secret to significance—a life *full* of God. A life *steeped* in the things of God. A life overflowing with the attributes, pursuits, and purposes of God.

I wonder if this is how you would describe your life. Overflowing with God.

I sat by a guy on an airplane one time who compared his relationship with God to Red Bull. Whenever he needs a boost or pick-me-up, he gets some God. That's how he described it.

"I love to get churched-up!"

He said that about thirty times in the two-hour flight. And I admit, God can be very exciting. And God can lift your spirits. But it made me wonder how God feels about occupying that particular role in the man's life. I know what my wife would say if I interacted with her like that. If I only go to Ginny when I need a boost or a little pick-me-up, if I only give her attention when I want something, need something, or crave something I can't get on my own—we don't believe in divorce…*but*…I don't think we'd stay married. Period.

Unfortunately, the guy on the plane isn't the only one who treats God like a can of Red Bull. Maybe it's how you interact with God. I'm a pastor. I talk about Jesus for a living. I'm supposed to say *Jesus* as the answer to every question, but I know I don't always hit the target in my life. And I didn't always organize my life around the things of God. In fact, I lived lots of life *seeking first* the kingdom of *me, myself, and I.*

"I was born to do these things!"

That's what my friend said as we jogged across the field by my parents' house. Well, I was jogging. Justin was philosophizing about his reason for being as he casually dribbled a soccer ball. It was the same field I first played soccer on. Now, it was eighteen years later. It was the off-season, a few weeks after our first year as professional soccer players ended.

"I was born to have this ball at my feet," Justin says.

I couldn't disagree. I always felt I was *born* to play soccer. It was my dream from the very first moment I stood on the exact same field, from the moment I saw all the kids running, screaming, and kicking each other. I knew.

I believe God birthed the vision in me. I believe God has given you specific talents, abilities, and passions too. It's like Howard Thurman, the twentieth-century civil rights activist and key mentor to Martin Luther King, Jr., once said:

> Don't ask yourself what the world needs, ask yourself what makes you come alive. And then go and do that. Because what the world needs is people who have come alive.[120]

Soccer made me come *alive*. Soccer was my passion. Soccer opened doors for me. Here's the problem: for many years, soccer was only about *me*.

My glory.

My advancement.

My popularity.

My purpose.

Even when I met Jesus at age eighteen, soccer was *my* thing. I once told a friend, "I'll keep soccer. God can have everything else."

I wonder if you ever think like that. Do you ever view your work as separate from God? Do you ever view your hobbies as separate from God? What about your expense claims? Taxes? Business expenses? Golf score? The question is: Do you ever compartmentalize your life?

I've noticed it's easy to think certain things are yours and certain things are God's. Maybe you're like I was. You've given God 90 percent of your life. By comparison, it's excellent. As you look around, few others match your commitment. And it might not be a conscious thing. You might *think* you're all in. You might think God is your top priority. But look at your three T's: time, talent, and treasure—they'll tell you where your real priorities are. They will also tell you what you pursue most.

"I was born to do these things!" Justin says.

"So was I," I respond. I just had the reason upside-down at the time.

I wanted to be famous.

I wanted to be rich.

I wanted to drive a Pontiac Firebird Trans Am.

But it never satisfied. The pursuit was never enough. I could never figure out *why* I had so much of what I wanted, but I never felt fulfilled.

In many parts of Africa, the church tells people *when you repent of your sin, you must repent of your sport.* A pastor in Nigeria once told me directly, *soccer is evil.* He's not the only pastor I've talked with who believes soccer is corrupt. After all, it's filled with lying, cheating, and lots of unnecessary flopping and flailing on the ground. It's true. The flopping and flailing part. Especially if you're Italian. But it doesn't mean you can't play soccer for the purpose of God.

I know questionable bankers, entrepreneurs, dentists and…even *pastors* too. It doesn't mean banking, business, or beautiful teeth are corrupt. It just means some people have the wrong purpose.

I wanted to be famous.

I wanted to be rich.

I wanted to drive a Pontiac Firebird Trans Am.

It just never satisfied.

But one day, standing on the side of a dirt field in Zimbabwe, I discovered that if you want life to the full, a life of significance, a life that satisfies more than you can imagine, you don't have to change your pursuit, you just need to change your reason. You can still be a banker, an entrepreneur; you can even be a dentist, if you want. You just need the right reason. Here's how I like to say it: No matter what you do, become rich toward God.

◎ ◎ ◎

Jesus once told a story about a wedding banquet. Here's how it begins:

> "The kingdom of heaven is like a king who prepared a wedding banquet for his son. He sent his servants to those who had been invited to the banquet to tell them to come, but they refused to come.
>
> "Then he sent some more servants and said, 'Tell those who have been invited that I have prepared my dinner: My oxen and fattened cattle have been butchered, and everything is ready. Come to the wedding banquet.'
>
> "But they paid no attention and went off—one to his field, another to his business."[121]

Here's a summary: the king threw a party. The king invited guests. The guests refused to come. In fact, *they paid no attention* to the king; *they went off—one to his field, another to his business.*

It's how we interact with God.

In the original language, the idea isn't as harsh as it's presented here. The idea has more to do with distraction. You could say it like this: the guest's attention was *elsewhere.* It's not that the majority of guests ignored the invitation flat-out. They didn't actually reject the king; they were just *distracted* by the busyness of life.

They went off—one to his field, another to his business.

I wonder if this ever happens to you. Does the busyness of life ever captivate your attention? Kids, chores, jobs, fixing stuff, cleaning stuff, changing stuff…there's plenty to do. And then there's God. He wants to be your priority. He wants to be your purpose. He wants to be your pursuit. Here's how Jesus says it:

> You did not choose me, but I chose you and appointed you so that you might go and bear fruit— fruit that will last—and so that whatever you ask in my name the Father will give you.[122]

Jesus wants to give us what we need. He actually wants to provide far more than we expect. The problem is that *we're distracted*. We give priority to the stuff of life instead of the one who gives it. I do it all the time.

I wonder if God ever sits back at laughs. Not that our preoccupation is comical, but life to the full is so simple, and we make it complex. But we look for gaps. We look for pockets of time. We try to squeeze God into the little holes in our life. Driving to work, we toss up a prayer. Riding the stationary bike at the gym, we read the *verse of the day* on our Bible app. Silence? It's non-existent. Solitude? What's that? We're always in motion. Always going. Always doing. And we fit God in where we can.

I love what John Mark Comer says in his overly convicting book *The Ruthless Elimination of Hurry*:

Maybe that's why God eventually has to command the Sabbath. Does that strike you as odd? It's like commanding ice cream or live music or beach days. You would think we'd all be chomping at the bit to practice the Sabbath. But apparently there's something about the human condition that makes us want to hurry our way through life as fast as we possibly can, to rebel against the limitations of time itself.[123]

I told you. *Convicting.*

God is throwing a party. God has invited you. God wants you to come. The question is: What do you prioritize? God…or everything else?

◎ ◎ ◎

You've probably heard of Air Force One, the aircraft designated to carry the President of the United States. Have you heard of the presidential yacht—the USS Potomac? Well, technically, the Potomac only served as the yacht to President Franklin D. Roosevelt. It sank in the San Francisco Bay in 1980.[124]

Every President of the United States might not have a yacht, but it's widely known that FDR loved boating. Perhaps it's why he once made this comment:

> "To reach a port, we must sail—sail, not tie at anchor—sail, not drift."[125]

To be direct: you never *drift* to your destination.

It's true of sailing. It's true of significance. It's true of God.

No one drifts to life overflowing with God.

Emeritus Professor of New Testament and cofounder of The Gospel Coalition, D. A. Carson says it like this:

> People do not drift toward holiness. Apart from grace-driven effort, people do not gravitate toward godliness, prayer, obedience to Scripture, faith, and delight in the Lord. We drift toward compromise and call it tolerance; we drift toward disobedience and call it freedom; we drift toward superstition and call it faith. We cherish the indiscipline of lost self-control and call it relaxation; we slouch toward prayerlessness and delude ourselves into thinking we have escaped legalism; we slide toward godlessness and convince ourselves we have been liberated.[126]

We simply do not drift toward God. I think it's why the apostle Paul warns, "Be very careful, then, how you live—not as unwise but as wise."[127]

Be very careful how you live.

I wish someone had posted that in the watch store I visited two weeks ago, at least the part about being *very careful*. It was a routine trip. My son Noah and I went to buy Ginny a birthday present. I had been in the same store a few weeks prior with Ginny, trying to get a feel for what she would like.

"Oh, is this your son?!" says the well-dressed middle-aged woman at the counter.

Noah is sprinting around the store shouting, "I like this one. No, I like this one. No, I like this one!"

"Um, well, yeah…this is he," I say, with a bashful smile.

The woman was very gracious. There was a well-dressed middle-aged man working as well. So, we're all talking about the watch my wife likes when Noah runs up behind me and jumps onto my waist.

Think of the absolute most embarrassing moment you've ever had in your entire life. That was this moment for me. Two weeks ago. Standing in the watch store. I'm sure it wasn't premeditated, but Noah pulled my running shorts, and underwear, down below my knees.

I wish I could say I was able to pull everything right back into place, but Noah was hanging on my waist.

Be very careful how you live. Pay attention to what you do, and the things happening around you.

I think it's what Jesus is saying when he talks about the person who calls to God at the end of their life. "Lord, Lord," this person says, "let me into heaven." Here's how Jesus puts it:

> I can see it now—at the Final Judgment thousands strutting up to me and saying, "Master, we preached the Message, we bashed the demons, our super-spiritual projects had everyone talking." And do you

know what I am going to say? "You missed the boat. All you did was use me to make yourselves important. You don't impress me one bit."[128]

I think this will happen more than we expect. Athletes will tell Jesus about how they scored touchdowns and pointed toward the sky. Politicians will tell Jesus they thanked him in speeches. Entrepreneurs will talk about money they donated to charities doing good works. But God really isn't interested in lip service. God wants your heart. God wants your life.

◎ ◎ ◎

So, maybe you're ready to pursue significance. Maybe you're unwilling to miss God's best. It's not where I started, but standing on the soccer field in Africa, I finally decided, *I don't want to miss my life*! Do you? Consider the rich fool. Jesus tells his story:

> The ground of a certain rich man yielded an abundant harvest. He thought to himself, "What shall I do? I have no place to store my crops."
>
> Then he said, "This is what I'll do. I will tear down my barns and build bigger ones, and there I will store all my surplus grain."[129]

It's a very simple story. It's a common way to think. *What I have is good, but bigger is better…newer is nicer.* I've been there. I think that. But Jesus says two words to the rich man you never want to hear from God: "You fool."[130] Here's Jesus' unabridged response:

> "This very night your life will be demanded from you. Then who will get what you have prepared for yourself?" This is how it will be with whoever stores up things for themselves but is not rich toward God.[131]

So, here's the question: do you organize and prioritize your life around the things of God?

Remember, you need to look at your three T's—time, talent, and treasure. They tell you what you pursue most. But if you want to *become rich toward God*, here's a few ideas:

- PRAY: I once heard that the average Christian in America spends less than one minute praying each day. I don't know what the right amount of time to pray is, but if I only talked to my wife one minute a day, she won't talk back after a while. What if you made it your goal to talk to God like you talk to a friend—often, with enthusiasm, with the expectation that your interaction has purpose? I guarantee it will change your perspective. It will change your heart too.

- READ: Just 11 percent of Americans read the Bible daily.[132] I committed to the habit of reading God's Word daily over twenty years ago, and I'll be honest, most days I don't have a revelation. But it's all about the compound interest. James Clear makes it clear in his book Atomic Habits. "Every action you take is a vote for the type of person you wish to become. No single instance will transform your beliefs, but as the votes build up, so does the evidence of your new identity."[133] I'm certain you don't have to read the Bible to be a Christian, but if you want to be rich toward God, you do.

- INVEST: Mother Teresa once commented that being unloved without people to care for you is the worst disease that any human being can ever experience.[134] We'll pursue this idea more fully in the next chapter, but one of the fastest ways to become rich toward God is to invest your life in others.

- GIVE: There's a prophet in the Old Testament who gives some advice on how to use money. "Bring the whole tithe into the storehouse, that there may be food in my house. Test me in this," says the LORD Almighty, "and see if I will not throw open the floodgates of heaven and pour out so much blessing that there will not be room enough to store it."[135] I don't know about you, but I'm interested in this type of blessing from God. Generosity is something we must intentionally cultivate. It's like significance; you never drift to a generous life. And how we use our money isn't the only aspect of generosity, but it does say something about our heart. We'll flesh this out in the final chapter, but this is a prerequisite to becoming rich toward God: give your life away.

- BEHOLD: Scientists have discovered that thoughts travel along specific pathways to various destinations in our brains. As we consider the same thought frequently, the pathway for that thought becomes more deeply entrenched. Here's the final result: the more often we contemplate something, the more it will affect our thought patterns, how we feel, and how we behave. Here's how English poet, William Blake put it: "We become what we behold."[136] The more you behold God, the more you grow in the things of God. The more you consider the things of God, the more you become rich toward God. Another British author, Alan Redpath, says it like this: "Look up into his lovely face and as you behold him, he will transform you into his likeness. You do the beholding—he does the transforming."[137] If you want to become rich toward God make it your goal to behold him each day.

I'm not sure if the centenarians from Okinawa, Sardinia, Nicoya, Icaria, or the Seventh-day Adventists in Loma Linda, California, practice these habits daily, but I'm guessing they do. It's the *Blue Zone* discovery. God adds life to your life.

No one ever drifts to significance.

No one ever stumbles into life to the full.

You choose your target.

Alfred Nobel made that discovery in 1888. I discovered the same thing one hundred years later.

God is throwing a party. God has invited you. God wants you to come. The question is: What do you prioritize? God? Or everything else?

You choose.

Chapter 8

BECOME RICH IN COMMUNITY

Life is not meant to be lived alone.

Every Spanish sailor would agree.

Here's an example: The year is 1956, and a Peruvian boat is sailing off the coast of South America. The boat is heading toward an inlet of the Amazon River when it comes to a strange sight: a small Spanish boat is anchored off the coast. The crew of Peruvian sailors peer across the ocean, and they notice a solitary Spanish sailor stretched out on the deck of the boat.

"Can we help you?"

That's what the Peruvians begin to shout seeing the Spanish sailor; his eyes are blood shot, his skin is burned, his lips are parched and swollen.

The Spaniard is literally dying of thirst.

"Water! Water! I need fresh water," the Spaniard says.

Surprised by the request, the Peruvians instruct the

Spaniard to lower his bucket and help himself. Fearing he's been misunderstood, the Spaniard shouts back, "No! I need *fresh* water!" Again, the Peruvians instruct the Spaniard to lower his bucket and help himself. It seems obvious to the group of Peruvians. It seems straightforward. But sitting on his boat, all alone, dying of thirst, the Spanish sailor doesn't realize he is anchored in the mouth of the Amazon River. He doesn't realize he has access to all the fresh water he could want.[138]

Seventeenth-century English poet John Donne captures the essence of this scenario with the title of his famous poem, "No man is an island."[139]

Whether you're an English poet, a Spanish fisherman, or *anyone* else, at some point, somehow, some way, you learn: life is not meant to be lived alone.

I like to think I'm self-sufficient. I've always been this way. My mom tells a different story. She loves to remind me of my first report card.

"Plays well with others, not by himself."

That was the comment my teacher made on my first report card in kindergarten. Of course, there are no grades in kindergarten, so the comment was significant. At least, that's what my mom says.

Maybe you're like me. You think you're self-sufficient. Maybe you *are* self-sufficient. Maybe you don't need other people to accomplish most of your goals. Honestly, I often feel like that. But I've learned, life to the full only happens in community. Here's how Tim Keller says it:

> Ultimate reality is a community of persons who know and love one another. That is what the universe, God, history, and life is all about. If you favor money, power, and accomplishment over human relationships, you will dash yourself on the rocks of reality.[140]

I tried to communicate this idea to my five-year-old son last Christmas.

"I can do it myself!"

That was the first thing Noah said as he arrived at the bottom of the stairs, hours before sunrise on Christmas morning. There were presents everywhere. The Christmas tree lights were on. Noah's first bike stood out amongst all the other gifts.

"I don't need help. I can do it all by myself," he says.

He hadn't even approached the bike. He just stood there, shouting; looking at his brand-new, bright red bike, with the super cool yellow racing stripes down the sides and the number plate strapped to the handlebars. Apparently, he noticed the training wheels as well.

Now pointing, still refusing to approach the bike, Noah says, "What are those?"

"Training wheels," I say.

"I don't need training; I want to ride myself," he shouts.

We had a separate conversation about gratitude and appreciation later. But Noah represents how many of us approach life. We think:

I can do it myself.

I don't need help.

And maybe you don't *need* help. Maybe you *can* accomplish all your goals, and all your hopes, and all your dreams on your own. There are people who have proven it's possible. There are people everywhere working, playing, vacationing, and living life alone. Just look around. You don't have to convince me that you *can* do it yourself, that you don't need help. It's possible. But not if significance is the target of your life.

◎ ◎ ◎

Let's revisit the man called *lame.*

Remember the guy from Mark 5 who hung out at the pool in Jerusalem for thirty-eight years? Jesus walked up to this guy lying by the pool, and he says, "Do you want to get well?" No small talk. No formalities. No introduction. Just a question. Remember what the man called lame says:

> "Sir," the invalid replied, "I have no one to help me into the pool when the water is stirred. While I am trying to get in, someone else goes down ahead of me."

I have no one to help me.

That's what the man called lame says to Jesus.

It's why he can't advance.

It's why he can't move on.

It's why he's still sitting at the pool thirty-eight years later. But what about the angel who stirred the water? Remember the angel? Once a day the angel would stir up the water and the first person to jump in was healed of whatever disease they had. I failed high school geometry… *twice*…but my calculator app says that the man called lame had 13,870 opportunities to jump into the water first.

But he didn't.

Maybe the angel only came once a week? The verse omitted from many Bibles says the angel came every day, but maybe the angel came less often. Maybe the angel only came every other day. Who knows? But let's just say the angel only came once a month, that's still 456 opportunities the man called lame would have to jump into the pool first.

But he didn't.

I have no one to help me, he said.

It feels like an excuse. That's what I've always thought as I've read this story; the man called lame is just trying to defend his position. I've always thought this guy could find a way into the water somehow. With all the opportunities, he could have jumped in first, if he really wanted to. But right from the beginning, here's what God says:

"It is not good for the man to be alone."[141]

Solomon, the wise king, says something similar:

> Two people are better off than one, for they can help
> each other succeed. If one person falls, the other can
> reach out and help. But someone who falls alone
> is in real trouble. Likewise, two people lying close
> together can keep each other warm. But how can
> one be warm alone? A person standing alone can be
> attacked and defeated, but two can stand back-to-
> back and conquer.[142]

Apparently, we are better together. We need each other. It's
a good idea. But it's also God's best plan for our life.

Do you know there are fifty-four "one anothers" in the
New Testament? I won't list them all, but here are a few:
Love *one another*.[143] Be devoted to *one another*.[144] Live
in harmony with *one another*.[145] Bear with *one another*.[146]
Show kindness to *one another*.[147] And I love this one...
"Outdo *one another* in showing honor."[148]

It's like a competition.

Outdo one another in showing honor.

I often wonder what would happen if *one another* was a
greater priority for more of us. I wonder what would happen if we were actually for *one another*—if that were our
goal. I wonder, how important *one another* is to you.

I think this emphasis on life with *one another* was the

problem for the man called lame. Think about it. The guy had been at the pool for thirty-eight years. So, his life was at the pool. Everyone he knew was at the pool. I'm sure his friends were at the pool. But here's the question: Were his friends focused on *one another*, or were they focused on themselves? The answer seems obvious.

I have no one to help me, he said.

We are designed for relationships. If you're an introvert, that statement might make you cringe, but it's true no matter how you're wired. Consider the research.

Dozens of studies reveal that people who have social support from family, friends, and their community are happier, healthier, and live longer. One study found that people with strong social relationships have a 50 percent lower rate of mortality than those with poor social interactions.[149] Other studies connect the lack of social ties to depression, later-life cognitive decline, and premature death—it's an effect on mortality risk comparable to smoking fifteen cigarettes a day; it's a greater risk than obesity and physical inactivity.[150]

In his book *Timeless: Nature's Formula for Health and Longevity*, Louis Cozolino, professor of psychology at Pepperdine University, makes a significant observation. He writes:

Of all the experiences we need to survive and thrive, it is the experience of relating to others that is the most meaningful and important. A lifestyle that maximizes social interaction and human-to-human contact is good for the brain at every stage, particularly for the aging brain.[151]

Dr. Brené Brown, Huffington Foundation Endowed Chair at The Graduate College of Social Work at the University of Houston, makes a similar suggestion:

A deep sense of love and belonging is an irreducible need of all men, women, and children. We are biologically, cognitively, physically, and spiritually wired to love, to be loved, and to belong. Without healthy connection, the result is not simply a quieter, duller life. The outcome is much worse than that. When these needs are not met, we don't function as we were meant to. We break. We fall apart. We grow numb. We ache. We hurt others. We get sick. There are certainly other causes of illness, numbness, and hurt, but the absence of love and belonging will always lead to suffering.[152]

We are wired to love, to be loved, and to belong.

It's why I'm here.

It's why you're here.

It's the secret to significance.

If you want life to the full, you must become rich in community.

◎ ◎ ◎

A few weeks ago, I asked a very innocent question while preaching. Well, I thought it was innocent. Here it is. I asked everyone sitting in the audience: Have you ever been *stoned* on your way to church? One woman came up to me after the service and told me about her experience as a child of the sixties. I think people misunderstood my question.

In the first-century Greco-Roman World, followers of Jesus were often beaten, imprisoned, and stoned for their faith. It was a common theme. Followers of Jesus were persecuted. It wasn't ideal, but it was universal. It's within this context that the apostle Paul wrote. Here's what he says:

> Let us consider how we may spur one another on toward love and good deeds, not giving up meeting together, as some are in the habit of doing, but encouraging one another—and all the more as you see the Day approaching.[153]

Several other translations say it like this:

"Let us *consider* one another…"

It seems upside-down or backward or, as my British friends like to say, *pear-shaped*. People are suffering.

People are dying. People are being abused because of their faith. And Paul says, here's what you do: *consider* one another. Maybe he meant to say: *Run! Hide! It's every man for himself!* That would make more sense. After all, the more public the first-century followers of Jesus were about their faith, the more they called attention to themselves, the more they were persecuted. And it seems Paul is saying *lean into it.*

In the original language, the word *consider* means: be attentive; be thoughtful. It means, take careful note of how others are doing.

It's Paul's instruction to followers of Jesus in the first-century Greco-Roman World.

It's Paul's instruction to us.

Take careful note of how others are doing.

It's how we progress. It's how we thrive. It's how we experience *life to the full.* Consider one another. But it's not natural. It's not the culture we live in. And unfortunately, it's not the culture of the church. So, maybe Paul should have said, consider yourself. Consider your own situation. Consider your own plight, your own problems, your own predicament—before you consider others. If Paul had said that, it might seem more feasible. I know this firsthand. But here's the problem: it's impossible to live for significance alone. It's like the process of sharpening iron.

In biblical times it was impossible for one tool to become sharper without the presence of another. Two blades would be dull and useless on their own. It's why King Solomon's illustration is so powerful: "As iron sharpens iron, so one person sharpens another."[154]

It seems obvious, but Solomon doesn't say iron sharpens itself. He doesn't say iron is sharpened all alone. Or as iron is isolated, individualistic, and reclusive…then it's sharpened.

Iron needs iron to be as sharp as it can be.

But we live in a culture that celebrates radical individualism. It's my way right away. It's my way or the highway. It's how we think. Well, everyone but Mother Teresa. As I mentioned in the previous chapter, she once famously commented: "Being unloved without people to care for you is the worst disease that any human being can ever experience." Maybe it's why Jesus teaches us to pray corporately? Here's what Jesus says:

> This, then, is how you should pray:
>
> Our Father in heaven,
>
> hallowed be your name,
>
> your kingdom come,
>
> your will be done on earth as it is in heaven.
>
> Give us today our daily bread.
>
> And forgive us our debts, as we also have forgiven our debtors.

And lead us not into temptation, but deliver us from the evil one.[155]

Have you ever noticed the overwhelming communal emphasis of this prayer?

Our Father…

Give *us*…

Forgive *us*…

Lead *us*…

Deliver *us*…

I don't know about you, but I've read this prayer, said this prayer, and thought about this prayer thousands of times. I studied this prayer in seminary. I memorized this prayer as a child. But still, so often, I pray: My Father…give me… forgive me…lead me…deliver *me. Me…me…me…me.*

Sixteenth-century English theologian John Wesley once put it like this: "The religion described by our Lord… cannot subsist without society." A common paraphrase of Wesley's point is there is no such thing as a solitary Christian.[156]

Maybe it's why first-century followers of Jesus living in the Greco-Roman World got stoned so often. Maybe it's not such a bad thing.

◎ ◎ ◎

As I write this, we're in the middle of a global pandemic—all of us. I'd like to believe it will end soon. I don't know. Here's what I do know:

- Over 50 percent of adults report their mental health has been negatively impacted because of COVID-19.

- In America, 36 percent of people are having significant sleep issues.

- Thirty-two percent of people are overeating.

- Over 30 percent of people say they currently have symptoms of anxiety or depression.

This is in addition to things like stress-related disorders, substance abuse, divorce, and suicide, which have all sky-rocketed during the pandemic.[157] Research suggests there are several reasons for this response, but one stands out—social distance.

Terms like "shelter in place," "self-quarantine," and "social bubble" have become standard. In prison, people get sent to *isolation* for poor behavior; in a global pandemic, it's self-imposed. Here's the point: social distance might be good for physical health during a global pandemic, but it's detrimental to everything else, including your spiritual well-being. King Solomon puts it like this: "Whoever *isolates* himself seeks his own desire; he breaks out against all sound judgment."[158] Here's Jesus' invitation:

"Are you tired? Worn out? Burned out on religion? Come to me…Keep company with me and you'll learn to live freely and lightly."[159]

Come to me.

Keep company with me.

It's Jesus' invitation—he wants a relationship with us. He also wants relationships *for* us. It's how we're designed. It's part of our purpose. It's how we experience *life to the full*— pursue a relationship with God and others. The Christian faith requires community. I appreciate how Timothy Paul Jones articulates this point: "I cannot follow Jesus alone any more than I can get married alone."[160]

And maybe you feel it would be better to be *married alone*; if so, the best marriage counselor I know sits one door down from my office, but still, it's not God's best plan for your life.

We are social beings.

Rob Cross, the Edward A. Madden Professor of Global Leadership at Babson College makes this observation:

> Many of us strive for a meaningful job, an impressive title, or a sizable salary at the ideal company. In doing so, we drastically undervalue the importance of relationships, even though extensive research shows that it's people, not the perfect job, that lead to fulfillment.[161]

It's people, not the perfect job, that lead to fulfillment. People, not possessions. People, not prosperity or property or pastimes or Porsche convertibles (ok, it just felt like I needed one more "P"), but we are designed for relationships. So, no matter what you have or what you get or what you want or what you pursue…if you don't become rich in community, you might be successful, but you won't be fulfilled.

Let me give you ten reasons to become rich in community. These aren't necessarily found in Scripture, but they are based on research, so I'd like to believe Jesus would agree. Here they are:

1. Live longer

2. Have fewer health problems

3. Be happier

4. Feel wealthier

5. Decrease stress

6. Have a greater sense of purpose

7. Have higher self-esteem

8. Have lower anxiety and depression

9. Have a greater sense of belonging

10. Feel more fulfilled[162]

I don't know about you, but I'd choose any of these options. And it's not like I'm suggesting a poke in the eye with a sharp stick in exchange. You just need to consider others. That is, if significance is your goal.

◎ ◎ ◎

I wonder what might have happened if the man called lame had people in his life who *considered* him. Do you think he would have sat at the pool for thirty-eight years? Do you think he would have been an invalid? Do you think he would have been *lame*?

It seems so simple: invest in others like you want them to invest in you. Isn't that some sort of gold-plated *rule*? Don't we all learn that at the same time as the ABCs? It seems fundamental. It seems foundational. It seems obvious. But we live in a culture that's primarily thoughtful, attentive, and takes careful note of…*self*.

So, let's say you want to be different. Let's say you decide to pursue the interests of others like you pursue your own. What would that look like? How can you actually become rich in community? Here are a few ideas:

1. Add value: Start each day thinking about how to add value to the lives of those around you. Ask yourself, *What am I going to do to add value to the lives of others today?* This exercise doesn't need to be long. But the more you consider how to add value to those around you, the more likely you are to do it.

2. Pray: I've noticed it's very difficult to dislike people whom you pray for often. In fact, the more you pray for others, the more you will want to see them succeed. Here's a challenge: pray for other people more than you pray for yourself. Try it. It's a good guide for how to pray.

3. Serve: Look for people who need help. At first you might feel there's no one around you who really *needs* help, but keep looking. The more you serve, the more others-centered you become. Look to serve one new person every day. It doesn't need to be at a Saturday Soup Kitchen. Hold the door. Buy someone coffee. Volunteer at church. Join the school board. We'll talk about this in depth in the last chapter; it's essential to experiencing life to the full.

4. Choose second: It's not my natural inclination (I'm not sure it's anyone's), but look for ways to choose second every day. Let someone go ahead of you in line at the grocery store. Let your colleague have the last drink in the staff refrigerator. Take the seat with limited view at the game. These don't need to be great acts of faith, but the more you choose second, the more you place others in first.

5. Join a group: I don't know what you like to do, but there's a group for almost everyone. Our church has different Bible study groups and small groups, but we have affinity groups too. We have a

running group, a cross-fit group, a cooking group, a divorced persons group, a singles group, we even have a group for pickle ball…and the list goes on. If we don't have a group you like, here's our policy: create a new group! It's up to you to join.

◎ ◎ ◎

I don't know how invested in other people you are, but I know life is not meant to be lived alone.

We are designed for relationships.

We are social beings.

We are here for one another.

It's why Jesus questioned the man called lame.

I have no one to help me, he said.

I wonder, what would you say?

Chapter 9

GIVE YOUR LIFE AWAY

Former President of the Indian National Congress, Mahatma Gandhi, left his home in Mumbai in August of 1888. He traveled to England. He went to study law at the University of London.

As the story goes, one day Gandhi was standing on the platform at a train station waiting for a train, but when the train finally arrived…it didn't stop…it only slowed down as it passed through the station. Unfortunately, the British Rail Company had a policy in those days that they would only stop if there were *white* passengers waiting at the station.

But Gandhi really wanted to get on the train.

So, Gandhi started to sprint as fast as he could. The train was *literally* passing him by as he leaped over the train track into the last car on the train. It felt like success. It felt like victory. But here's the problem, Gandhi's shoe slipped off his foot. It was one shoe, to be exact. It fell onto the train track.

I don't know what you would do if you lost a shoe

jumping onto a train, but Gandhi immediately reached down, grabbed his other shoe, and threw that shoe onto the train track as well. A perplexed onlooker approached Gandhi a few minutes later. He wanted to know why Gandhi had thrown his other shoe onto the train track. Here's Gandhi's response: "The one who finds my shoe shall now have a pair."[163]

It's the perspective of a man who understands the secret to significance. It's the perspective of a man who gave his life to serve others. And it might not be your first thought, but if you want *life to the full* you must give your life away.

I don't remember much from the 80s. Most of that's intentional. I do remember this bumper sticker. I think it was on a coffee mug too. It said, "He who dies with the most toys wins."[164]

I liked that thought…*in the 80s.*

It felt aspirational.

It felt competitive.

It felt like a compelling vision for life.

Malcolm Forbes, the flamboyant billionaire and publisher of *Forbes Magazine*, coined the phrase. It's probably why Forbes owned castles, hot air balloons, yachts, motorcycle racing teams, and the island of Laucala in Fiji. Forbes once paid over a million dollars for an egg.[165] It's a special egg, I guess. It was created in St. Petersburg, Russia. It's adorned with jewelry. It's called Fabergé. It's still just an egg.

I wonder if Malcolm Forbes still believes his mantra, post-humously. I wonder if he actually believed his mantra while he was alive. I also wonder, did Malcolm Forbes ever meet Winston Churchill? Here's what Churchill said: "We make a living by what we get; we make a life by what we give."[166]

It's similar to what Gandhi says: "The best way to find yourself is to lose yourself in the service of others."[167]

Let's consider the research.

Scientific evidence shows that giving to others increases the quality of our life. Apparently, our brains are hard-wired to serve.

"You gotta see this!"

It's what Jorge Moll wrote in an email to his colleague Jordan Grafman. They were neuroscientists at the National Institutes of Health. They had been scanning the brains of volunteers who were asked to think about a scenario involving the choice to donate a sum of money to charity or keep it for themselves. The results of the research were staggering.

In the mid-2000s Grafman led a study that examined brain impulse, specifically, where in the brain the impulse to *give* originates. The objective of the research was to understand why it feels so good to help others. The study was simple. People were asked to make donations to charities. The researchers then examined the test subjects'

resulting brain activity using functional magnetic reso-
nance imaging (fMRI), which creates images of the brain's
activity by detecting physical changes, such as blood
flow, resulting from the activity of neurons. The team of
researchers also considered everyday behaviors as they
sought to link the results of the imagining experiments
with the subjects' regular involvement in charitable work.

In her book *The Giving Way to Happiness*, Jenny Santi captures the scenario well. Here's what Santi writes:

> Grafman was more interested in what happened
> when subjects donated or opposed donation at a cost
> to themselves. The study involved nineteen people,
> each of whom had the potential to walk away with
> a pot of $128. They also were given a separate pool
> of funds, which they could choose to distribute to
> a variety of charities linked to controversial issues,
> such as abortion, euthanasia, nuclear power, war
> and the death penalty. A computer presented each
> charity to the subjects in a series and gave them the
> option to donate, to oppose donation, or to receive
> a payoff, adding money to the pot. Sometimes, the
> decision to donate or oppose was costly, calling for
> subjects to take money out of the pot. They gave an
> average of $51 from the pot and pocketed the rest.

> It turned out that a similar pattern of brain activ-
> ity was seen when subjects chose either to donate
> or to take a payoff. In either case, an area of the
> brain toward the forehead, known as the anterior

prefrontal cortex, lit up. When Dr. Grafman and his team asked subjects to rate their charitable involvement in everyday life, he found that those with the highest ratings also had the highest level of activity in the prefrontal cortex.

The results demonstrated that when the volunteers placed the interests of others before their own, the generosity activated a primitive part of the brain that usually lights up in response to food or sex. Donating affects two brain "reward" systems working together: the midbrain VTA (ventral tegmental area)…which also is stimulated by food, sex, drugs and money; as well as the subgenual area, which is stimulated when humans see babies and romantic partners.[168]

Here's what science tells us: we're hard wired to give; it's part of our genetic pre-disposition. It's also God's best plan for our life.

◎ ◎ ◎

"Give me $500 dollars."

That's what the police officer said to my friend, Phil, standing over Phil's car on the side of the road. It was the middle of the day. Phil was visiting a different city on business. The police officer said he pulled him over because he was driving erratically.

"Have you been drinking?" the police officer says.

"No! It's the middle of the day. I'm here on business, officer," Phil says.

"Give me $300 dollars."

The police officer was now speaking softer. He was leaning through the window of Phil's car. "You're going to jail if you don't give me $300 dollars," the police officer says.

"For what? I've done nothing wrong. I've broken no law," Phil says.

Clearly disturbed, the police officer was now walking around Phil's car. He kicks a tire. He slams his fist on the trunk door. Several minutes pass by. Phil is still sitting in the car.

"Ok, here's my final offer," the police officer says. "Do you see that McDonald's down the road?"

"Yes," Phil says.

"Buy me a Happy Meal, and I'll let you go. If not, you're going to jail," says the officer.

Phil didn't buy the Happy Meal, but I wonder if you've ever been in a scenario like this. It didn't happen in the United States. And it wasn't ethical. But let's disregard that. Here's the question: have you ever felt pressured to *give*? Maybe it wasn't money; it might have been time. Maybe it wasn't a police officer; it might have been your pastor. Here's the point: giving should be done freely. King Solomon says it like this:

"One person gives freely, yet gains even more;
another withholds unduly, but comes to poverty.
A generous person will prosper; whoever refreshes
others will be refreshed."[169]

A generous person will prosper.

It's not a suggestion.

It's a promise from God.

In the language of the Old Testament, this word, *prosper*, means "to make successful; to thrive; to flourish." It's the word *dashen* in Hebrew. It literally means "to be fat, grow fat, or to become fat."[170] It's not necessarily a desirable option in American culture—to become fat. But this is the biblical picture of prosperity…that you would literally be so filled up that you'd become bloated with the blessings of God. It's God's promise. It's what God wants for you. Eugene Peterson's translation of the above verses from Psalms provides an excellent summary:

> The world of the generous gets larger and larger;
>
> the world of the stingy gets smaller and smaller.
>
> The one who blesses others is abundantly blessed;
>
> those who help others are helped.[171]

Jesus says something similar: "Whoever has will be given more, and he will have an abundance. Whoever does not have, even what he has will be taken from him."[172]

It might seem contradictory? It might seem upside down? But this isn't just a spiritual idea. In their book *The Paradox of Generosity*, Christian Smith, a William R. Kenan, Jr., professor of sociology and the director of the Center for the Study of Religion and Society at the University of Notre Dame, and Hilary Davidson, PhD candidate in sociology at the University of Notre Dame, state:

> Generosity is paradoxical. Those who give receive back in turn. By spending ourselves for others' well-being, we enhance our own standing. In letting go of some of what we own, we better secure our own lives. By giving ourselves away, we ourselves move toward flourishing. This is not only a philosophical or religious teaching; it is a sociological fact.[173]

It's not just a religious idea.

It's not philosophical.

It's not just a way to get you to give something you really don't want to give. It's science. The more you give, the more you get. The more you serve, the more you are served. St. Francis of Assisi puts it like this: "For it is in giving that we receive."

God is a giver.

I'm sure you've seen the signs. Every Sunday, people hold them up in sports stadiums all around America. I often wonder if the people holding the signs are intoxicated…I'll leave that with the police officer who stopped my friend Phil in South Africa. Here's what the signs say:

> God so loved the world that he *gave* his one and only Son, that whosoever believes in him shall not perish but have eternal life.[174]

I see this verse on signs every time I watch professional football. I'm not sure why. I believe it though. The apostle Paul talks about the same thing: "He who did not spare his own Son, but *gave* him up for us all—how will he not also, along with him, graciously *give* us all things?"[175]

In the Bible, there's a lot of chat about what God *gave* and wants to *give*. Jesus talks about it too. Here's what Jesus says: "My purpose is to *give* them a rich and satisfying life."[176] I suppose you can dismiss the comment. I suppose you can ignore the offer. But not if you really believe that the *them* Jesus is talking about is *you*.

"My *purpose* is to give *you* a rich and satisfying life."

It's why Jesus came.

It's Jesus' purpose.

But Jesus could just as easily have said, "My purpose is to keep things from you." Right? Jesus could have said, "I came to deprive you; I came to hold back blessing; I came to limit your life." But that's not what Jesus says. The message of the gospel is that God gave *everything* for *you*.

God gave his own Son so that you can experience life to the full.

So, here's a question: Do you think it's possible to out-give God? (Maybe pause and think about that for a second.) Can you out-sacrifice God? What about this: Can you out-pace God if you try?

I confess, sometimes I think I can. It's not intentional, I assure you. But I've noticed, I often compartmentalize my life. Here's an example: I try to work out most days of the week. I'm a pastor. And I spend most of my time with people. So, I view the gym as *my* time. That's how I treat it, at least. I put my EarPods in. I crank the podcast. I jump on the machine. Ninety minutes later I walk out the door. It's my daily routine.

A few years ago, I joined a new gym. I was there six months before I realized I didn't know one person there. But maybe I wasn't supposed to? Maybe I don't need to give *my* time in the gym to God? That's what I thought. It's secretly what I wanted to believe. But I decided I better at least offer the gym to God in prayer. So, in between free weight flys and the rowing machine, I pray, "God, if you want my time in the gym, it's yours!"

I realize now that you shouldn't offer things you don't really want to give.

I walk into the gym the day after the first time I prayed this prayer, and while I'm changing, I notice a large pink bunny rabbit on my right deltoid. His purple friend was on the left. I immediately remember my friends' daughter adhering these *temporary* tattoos the night before. Of course, I didn't know anyone in the gym, so it didn't really matter. But apparently it did. The first person to walk past me was the largest guy in the gym. You know the one—his neck is bigger than your entire body—his hands look like giant slabs of meatloaf.

"Sweet bunnies, man!"

That's what the guy says to me as I walk by. I try to explain the situation. I try to justify my circumstance. He didn't seem to care.

"Sweet bunnies, man!"

He must have said it six times. It's actually the only thing he said to me that day. We did become friends though. A few weeks later, I gave him a Bible. A few weeks after that, he gave his life to Christ. Apparently, you can't out-give God. I've tried. But the more I give, the more I receive… *every time*. The more I serve others, the more I am served. I don't necessarily understand how it works, but I've learned, you really can't out-sacrifice or out-pace God. It's probably why Malachi suggests we should *test* God in giving. Here's what he says:

> "Bring the whole tithe into the storehouse, that there may be food in my house. Test me in this," says the Lord Almighty, "and see if I will not throw open the floodgates of heaven and pour out so much blessing that there will not be room enough to store it."[177]

I don't know about you, but this seems like a good offer. I'm all about *the floodgates of heaven* being opened and receiving *so much blessing* that I won't have enough room for it. I like to tell people, "I want everything God has for me and nothing he does not." It's not some health and wealth gospel belief. It doesn't mean you get everything you want or that life is perfect. But God extends an invitation to each of us.

Test me.

It's what God says.

Test me.

It's an invitation to see if you can out-give God. And it's not limited to finance. See if you can give too much of your talent away. Seriously. Try to do it. See if you can donate too much of your time. God invites you to try. Here's the invitation from my perspective: see if you can give more of your life away than God can give to you. Your motivation might not be altruistic at first. But that's ok. God is inviting you.

"You can have everything in life you want if you will just help enough other people get what they want."[178]

It's Zig Ziglar's famous principle.

It's the secret to significance: live to give your life away.

If I'm honest, I'm still working this out in my own life.

I wish I could say I've entirely mastered the art of living for others, but my old desire for success often shows up uninvited.

How can I add value to myself?

It's what success asks.

It's what I ask myself sometimes.

But here's what significance asks: *How can I add value to others?* I wonder if you ever ask yourself that question. How often do you consider others' needs before your own?

Consider this evolution from selfishness to significance: What can others do for me? → What can I do for myself? → What can I do for others? → What can I do *with* others for others?[179] Where do you fall on this continuum most of the time? As you look at your life, and you look at each day, what question do you most ask yourself?

There's a Chinese proverb that says, "If you continually give, you will continually have." A common rewording (sometimes attributed to Picasso) says it like this: "The meaning of life is to find your gift. The purpose of life is to give it away."[180] Philosophers, poets, and painters agree, but let's get back to the science. Have you heard of *helpers high*?

Twenty years ago, this term, *helpers high*, was introduced by volunteerism and wellness expert Allan Luks. It was his attempt to explain the powerful physical sensation associated with helping others, based on his research with over seventeen-hundred women who volunteered regularly. Luks studied the physical effects of giving, and his ground-breaking research revealed that over 50 percent of helpers reported feeling "high" when they helped others, while 43 percent felt stronger and more energetic.[181] It's similar to the experience of long-distance runners. Not that I've ever experienced it myself. I was a goalkeeper. But when running long distance, runners experience a high due to an increased endorphin release in the brain. It's physiological. It's scientifically proven. And giving has the same effect.

Giving makes you feel good, just like running. But research reveals several other benefits. Here are five:

1. *Giving makes us happy.* This is often referred to as *warm glow*. It's similar to helpers high. It's like eating chocolate. Who isn't happier after eating an entire bar of dark chocolate Ritter Sport (it's German—get on board!)? It's the finding of Jorge Moll and his colleagues at the National Institute of Health. People who give to charities activate regions of the brain associated with pleasure.[182] A 2008 study by Harvard Business School professor Michael Norton and his colleagues found that giving money to someone else lifted participants' happiness more than spending the money on themselves. And, happiness expert Sonja Lyubomirsky, a professor of psychology at the University of California, Riverside, saw similar results when she asked people to perform five acts of kindness each week for six weeks.[183]

2. *Giving is good for our health.* There's plenty of research that links varying forms of generosity to things like reduced blood pressure, less depression, less stress, and increased self-esteem. In his book *Why Good Things Happen to Good People*, Stephen Post, a professor of preventative medicine at Stony Brook University, reports that giving to others has been shown to increase health benefits in people with chronic illness, including HIV and multiple sclerosis.[184] Apparently, giving is extremely good for the aging population too. In a 1999 study led by Doug Oman of the University of California, Berkeley, they found that elderly people who volunteered for two or more organizations were forty-four percent less likely to die over a five-year period than were non-volunteers.[185]

3. *Giving promotes healing.* Experts call this *the wounded healer principle.* In a study of alcoholics going through the Alcoholics Anonymous program, those who helped others were nearly twice as likely to stay sober a year later, and their levels of depression were lower too.[186]

4. *Giving evokes gratitude.* I'm sure you've noticed, whether you give or receive a gift, you often feel a sense of gratitude. Research suggests this feeling promotes several positive results—you're more optimistic, you feel healthier, and you exercise more. In her book *Positivity*, Barbara Fredrickson, a pioneering happiness researcher, suggests that

cultivating gratitude in everyday life is one of the keys to increasing personal happiness. Fredrickson says, "When you express your gratitude in words or actions, you not only boost your own positivity but other people's as well."[187]

5. *Giving is contagious.* Generosity creates a ripple effect. A study by James Fowler of the University of California, San Diego, and Nicholas Christakis of Harvard, published in the *Proceedings of the National Academy of Science*, shows that when one person behaves generously, it inspires observers to behave generously later toward different people. In fact, the researchers found that altruism could spread by three degrees—from person to person to person to person.[188] They note, "Each person in a network can influence dozens or even hundreds of people, some of whom he or she does not know and has not met."[189]

Altruism spreads.

Generosity is a gift that keeps on giving.

Science says giving gives life to the giver.

But sometimes we think, *I can't afford to give; I don't have time; I don't have money; I don't have capacity to give.* Do you ever think like that? I don't know about you, but I do. I've got all these jobs, responsibilities, tasks, people, hobbies, and all the stuff of life I'm trying to manage, and I often find myself thinking, *I just can't afford to give any-thing more.*

I know all the buzz words and phrases, like "Blessed to be a blessing," and "Live to give." I attend conferences on gener-osity. I even write entire chapters about giving in books. But sometimes, if I'm honest, I still think—*I can't afford to give.*

Maybe you're like me. Just a little? If you are, here's a thought on giving. It comes direct from science: you can't afford *not* to give.

◎ ◎ ◎

He who dies with the most toys wins.

Maybe Malcolm Forbes was right.

Maybe the accumulation of *stuff* is a worthy pursuit.

Maybe getting everything you want is enough.

But what if it's not?

What if Forbes missed something?

What if you gain the world but you miss your life?

In his article *Giving Yourself Away*, Rusty Rustenbach makes this piecing remark:

> You and I live in an age when only a rare minority of individuals desire to spend their lives in pursuit of objectives which are bigger than they are…In our age, for most people, when they die it will be as though they never lived.[190]

It's the problem of success. It seems alluring. It seems worthwhile. It seems like a valid pursuit. But success is like the flowers of the field, here today, gone tomorrow. Significance is altogether different.

If you aim at significance, you might not collect as many toys. In fact, you might end up giving most of your toys away. But here's a thought: He who dies with the most toys still dies, and the toys don't go with him.

Epilogue

On Purpose

I am not famous.

I am not a multimillionaire.

I have never owned a black Pontiac Firebird Trans Am.

I am *satisfied* though.

I woke up this morning and ate oatmeal for breakfast. It's Thursday, so I took the trashcan to the curb for collection. I'll probably wash some things when I get home from work—clothes, dishes, cars, babies; you know, those type of things. Yesterday as I drove our son to soccer practice, I noticed the car was almost out of gas. I stopped at the nearest gas station I could find.

Glancing up from his iPad, as if it were a terrific inconvenience, Noah says, "Hey, what are you doing, Dad?"

"Pumping gas," I say.

I realize, my life might not always look like success. I

admit, somedays it doesn't *feel* like success. But on those days, I try to remember—success is not my goal.

◎ ◎ ◎

I climbed a mountain with my dad last year. The journey up Kilimanjaro is similar to life: it's easy until it's not.

Mt. Kilimanjaro is the highest peak in Africa: 19,341 feet above sea level. It takes five days to climb up, two days to climb down. You travel through all five vegetation zones of the earth on the journey.

Most days on Kilimanjaro felt like a long walk in the park to me. It was nice. It was beautiful. It wasn't overly taxing, that is, aside from the six-hours from summit base camp to the summit—those felt like the hardest, most difficult, *worst* six-hours of my life.

You attempt the summit at midnight; you climb entirely in the dark. And it's cold—like negative fifteen to negative thirty degrees Fahrenheit. And strange things happen when your brain doesn't have enough oxygen. The woman in front of me kept admiring the beauty of the trees, but there are no trees on the top of Mt. Kilimanjaro. And about an hour from the top, the guy behind me arbitrarily dove onto the ground. I tried to stay focused, but he pulled me down with him. Apparently, he saw a large bird flying toward our heads…no birds fly 19,341 feet high.

"I'll never, ever…*ever* do that again!"

That's what I told my wife upon descent.

"We'll see," she says, smiling. She knows me better than I know myself most of the time. I convinced three friends to climb Mt. Everest next year. Here's the point, there's only one way to the top of a very large mountain: one step at a time.

You never drift to the top of a mountain.

You never randomly arrive at the summit.

You make a choice.

You set a target.

And then you climb. It's similar to what my favorite Dutch priest, Henri Nouwen, says about joy:

> Joy does not simply happen to us. We have to choose joy and keep choosing it every day.[191]

> What good would it do to get everything you want and lose you, the real you?[192]

It's the question Jesus asks each of us.

It's the question I started answering twenty-five years ago. Standing on the side of the field. In the dirt. Watching African kids play soccer. I made a decision that totally reframed my perspective of *success*.

I didn't become a monk the day I decided to pursue significance. I didn't become a pastor or missionary that day either. I was a soccer player. It was my passion. It became my profession. I used soccer to fulfill my purpose for over twenty years.

Have you decided what the target of your life is?

I've learned that you can't do everything. You can't be all things to all people. You can't be everywhere at once. So, life is a series of choices. One yes is a hundred nos. Every activity we choose to invest in is a hundred activities we *can't* invest in.

In his famous memoir *Walden*, Henry David Thoreau hits the nail on the head, so to speak. He built a cabin in the woods and spent two years, two months and two days reflecting on life near Walden Pond. Here's what he says:

> I went to the woods because I wished to live deliberately, to front only the essential facts of life, and see if I could not learn what it had to teach, and not, when I came to die, discover that I had not lived.[193]

"When I came to die, discover that I had not lived." What a horrible thing to arrive at the end of life and realize you had never really *lived*. I've spent hours...*lots of hours*... considering that thought. But it's not Thoreau's best idea. This is:

Live deliberately.

I like to say it like this: on purpose. It's the metric I value most. It's the standard I measure each day by—am I *on purpose* or not?

Epilogue

◎ ◎ ◎

I don't know about you, but I don't want to just get by or just make it through. I don't want to keep my fingers crossed and grit my teeth to hopefully someday, somehow, with some luck limp across the finish line of life. I want a life of purpose. I want a life of meaning. I want *life to the full*. It's not the feeling you get when you've eaten too much turkey on Thanksgiving. That's not what Jesus is talking about.

Here's what the word *full* means in the original language: "exceeding expectation; beyond anticipation; over and above; more than necessary; exceedingly abundantly supreme."[194] It's the life Jesus has on offer. Life to the *full*. It's exceedingly, abundantly supreme.

Jesus offers a life of significance, but it doesn't just happen.

You choose it.

You make it your goal.

You aim at significance, and it's really not complex. Here's the secret to significance: organize and prioritize your life around the things that matter most—God, people, and service.

It might not be the American Dream.

It might not be what Sisyphus would do.

But I'm convinced of this: significance is success.

So, here's to the pursuit of significance. It might not be for everyone, but I think we should pursue it together.

One step at a time.

About the Author

Pastor. Author. Coach. Husband. Father. Friend. Aaron Tredway is passionate about living life to its fullest and pushing beyond the boundaries of everyday life through adventure.

As the vice president for Ambassadors Football International, Aaron has traveled to over 140 countries and has personally trained over five thousand soccer coaches in developing and emerging nations, teaching them how to create social impact and transformation through the platform of soccer.

In 2006, Aaron was the founder and executive director of the Cleveland City Stars, a professional soccer team. After a twenty-year professional soccer career as a player, coach, and executive, Aaron now serves as the lead pastor of Fellowship City Church, a growing multisite church in Cleveland, Ohio. Aaron is a sought-after speaker and consultant on the subject of leadership and has presented to several Fortune 500 companies. He also continues to mentor dozens of professional athletes around the world.

A graduate of Liberty University and California State University, Stanislaus, Aaron holds two degrees in physical education and two degrees in theology, including a doctorate of ministry.

Aaron published his first book, *To Who: A Competition for Glory*, in conjunction with the 2010 FIFA World Cup in South Africa. *To Who* has sold over one hundred thousand copies to date and has been published on three continents.

In 2016, Aaron released his second book, *Outrageous: Awake to the Unexpected Adventures of Everyday Faith*, which highlights Aaron's belief that we all have an opportunity to wake up to a life far more exciting than we imagine. He would much rather spend his time and energy traveling to the world's most remote, underserved areas with a soccer ball than lead a safe life without purpose.

He and his wife, Ginny, reside in Cleveland, Ohio, with their son, Noah.

Endnotes

Prologue

1   Mark 8:36 (MSG).

2   Esther 4:14 (NIV).

3   Jesse Carey, "12 of DL Moody's Most Profound Quotes about Faith," *Relevant* (website), February 5, 2016, https://www. relevantmagazine.com/faith/12-dl-moodys-most-profound-quotes-about-faith/. One of my favorite quotes ever!

4   John 10:10 (NIV).

5   John 10:10 (ESV).

6   John 10:10 (NLT).

7   John 10:10 (MSG).

Part One

Quote: Attributed to Jim Carrey.

Chapter 1

8   What do you want to know? You can find all sorts of fascinating stuff on Wikipedia! See Wikipedia, s.v. "Manchester," last modified September 8, 2021 at 00:27 (UTC), https:// en.wikipedia.org/wiki/History_of_Manchester#Etymology.

9   "Premier League Global Audience on the Rise," Premier League (website), July 16, 2019, https://www.premierleague.com/ news/1280062.

10   Deion Sanders, *Power, Money & Sex—How Success Almost Ruined My Life* (Nashville, TN: Thomas Nelson, 1999), 17.

11   Kobe Bryant, "In His Own Words," *Dime Magazine*, 2006.

12   Robert Goldman and Ronald Klatz, *Death in the Locker Room: Drugs and Sports*, second ed. (New York: Elite Sports Medicine Publications, 1992), 24.

13   Homer, *The Iliad*, trans. Robert Fagles, (New York: Penguin Classics, 1991), 10.497–503.

14   50 Cent, vocalist, "Outta Control," by Curtis James Jackson, Andre Young et al., released September 27, 2005, track 8 on *The Massacre*.

15   William James, *The Principles of Psychology*, vol. 1 (New York: Henry Holt and Company, 1890), 334.

16   C. S. Lewis, *The Weight of Glory* (New York: HarperCollins Publishers, 2015), 23.

17   Julia Naftulin, "Here's How Many Times We Touch Our Phones Every Day," *Insider* (website), July 13, 2016, https://www.businessinsider.com/dscout-research-people-touch-cell-phones-2617-times-a-day-2016-7.

18   Trevor Haynes, "Dopamine, Smartphones and You: A Battle for Your Time," *Science in the News* (website), Harvard Graduate School of the Arts and Sciences, May 1, 2018, https://sitn.hms.harvard.edu/flash/2018/dopamine-smartphones-battle-time/.

19   Jena Hilliard, "Social Media Addiction," *Addiction Center* (website), Recovery Worldwide, LLC, last edited August 30, 2021, https://www.addictioncenter.com/drugs/social-media-addiction/.

20   Philip Brickman and Donald T. Campbell, "Hedonic Relativism and Planning the Good Society," *Adaptation Level Theory: A Symposium*, ed. M. H. Appley (New York: Academic Press, 1971), 287–305.

21   "Mobile Fact Sheet," Pew Research Center, April 7, 2021, https://www.pewresearch.org/internet/fact-sheet/mobile/.

22   Jean-Jacques Rousseau, "Discourse on the Origin of Inequality," *The Discourses and Other Political Writings* (Cambridge, UK: Cambridge University Press, 1997), 165.

23   William Shakespeare, *Measure for Measure*, III.1.

24   Juliana Menasce Horowitz and Nikki Graf, "Most U.S. Teens See Anxiety and Depression as a Major Problem among Their Peers," Pew Research Center, February 20, 2019, https://www.pewresearch.org/social-trends/2019/02/20/most-u-s-teens-see-anxiety-and-depression-as-a-major-problem-among-their-peers/.

25   Jamie Ducharme, "A Lot of Americans Are More Anxious than They Were Last Year, a New Poll Says," *Time* (website), updated May 8, 2018, https://time.com/5269371/americans-anxiety-poll/.

26   Megan Leonhardt, "What You Need to Know about the Cost and Accessibility of Mental Health Care in America," Make It (website), CNBC LLC, May 10, 2021, https://www.cnbc.com/2021/05/10/cost-and-accessibility-of-mental-health-care-in-america.html.

27   Arthur C. Brooks, "'Success Addicts' Choose Being Special over Being Happy," *The Atlantic*, July 30, 2020, https://www.theatlantic.com/family/archive/2020/07/why-success-wont-make-you-happy/614731/.

28   Matthew Reitman, "Science Explains Why Winning the Lottery Won't Make You Happier," *Inside Hook* (website), February 27, 2017, https://www.insidehook.com/article/finance/science-explains-winning-lottery-wont-make-happier.

29   Will Chou, "I Am Rich, Successful, and Have Everything but Unhappy. Why? Science Reveals Answers," *Will You Laugh* (blog), August 7, 2020, https://willyoulaugh.com/i-am-rich-and-successful-but-not-happy.

30   Fyodor Dostoyevsky, *The House of the Dead or Prison Life in Siberia*, ed. Ernest Rhys (London: J. M. Dent & Sons, Ltd., 1911; Project Gutenberg, 2011), pt. 1, chap 2, https://www.gutenberg.org/files/37536/37536-h/37536-h.htm.

31   Heidi Grant Halvorson, PhD, "How to Keep Happiness from Fading," *Psychology Today*, August 15, 2012, https://www.psychologytoday.com/us/blog/the-science-success/201208/how-keep-happiness-fading.

32   Matthew 4:8 (NIV).

33   Matthew 4:9 (NIV).

34   Matthew 16:26 (HCSB).

35   John 10:10 (NIV).

Chapter 2

36   Laura Nash and Howard H. Stevenson, "Success that Lasts," *Harvard Business Review*, February 2004, https://hbr. org/2004/02/success-that-lasts.

37   "American Dream in American, n. and adj," OED Online, last modified September 2021, www.oed.com/view/Entry/6342.

38   *Merriam-Webster.com Dictionary*, s.v. "The American dream," accessed September 17, 2021, https://www.merriam-webster. com/dictionary/the%20American%20dream.

39   John F. Helliwell, Richard Layard et al., "World Happiness Report 2021," Sustainable Development Solutions Network, March 23, 2021, https://worldhappiness.report/ed/2021/.

40   "Americans Are the Unhappiest They've Been in 50 Years, Poll Finds," NBC News (website), June 16, 2020, https:// www.nbcnews.com/politics/politics-news/americans-are- unhappiest-they-ve-been-50-years-poll-finds-n1231153.

41   Kevin Rhea, "The Most Memorable Epocha, in the History of America," *The Housing Hour* (website), July 2, 2013, https://thehousinghour.com/general/ the-most-memorable-epocha-in-the-history-of-america/.

42   "The America Founding: Letter to Roger Weightman from Thomas Jefferson, June 24, 1826," School of Public Policy, Pepperdine University, accessed September 17, 2021, https:// publicpolicy.pepperdine.edu/academics/research/faculty- research/american-founding/important-documents/rogweight. htm.

43   James Truslow Adams, *The Epic of America* (Boston: Little Brown, 1931), 426.

44   Adams, *The Epic of America*, 124.

45   Adams, *The Epic of America*, xvi.

46   Sarah Churchwell, "A Brief History of the American Dream," The Catalyst: A Journal of Ideas from the Bush Institute, winter 2021, https://www.bushcenter.org/catalyst/state-of-the-american- dream/churchwell-history-of-the-american-dream.html.

47   Adams, *The Epic of America*, 406.

48   John Ortberg, *The Life You've Always Wanted: Spiritual Disciplines for Ordinary People* (Grand Rapids, MI: Zondervan, 2015), 77.

49   Matthew 5:3–10 (NIV).

50   C. S. Lewis, *God in the Dock*, (Grand Rapids, MI: Eerdmans, 1970), 181–82.

51   Psalm 16:11 (NKJV).

Chapter 3

52   Don't pretend you never heard of *Linsanity* circa 2011 New York Knicks—what a story! I hear he's a pretty great guy too.

53   Proverbs 27:20 (NLT).

54   2 Chronicles 9:13 (NIV).

55   Ecclesiastes 2:4–11 (MSG).

56   Henry George, *Progress and Poverty; an Inquiry into the Cause of Industrial Depressions and of Increase of Want with Increase of Wealth: the Remedy* (New York: AMS Press, 1973), 134.

57   CollinsDictionary.com, s.v. "success," accessed September 18, 2021, https://www.collinsdictionary.com/us/dictionary/english/success.

58   Albert Camus, *The Myth of Sisyphus* (New York: Knopf Doubleday, 2018), 120.

59   Matthew 16:26.

60   Alison Cashin, "The Children We Mean to Raise: The Real Messages Adults Are Sending about Values," *Making Caring Common Project*, Harvard Graduate School of Education, July 2014, https://mcc.gse.harvard.edu/reports/children-mean-raise.

61   Thomas Curran and Andrew P. Hill, "Perfectionism Is Increasing, and That's Not Good News," *Harvard Business Review*, January 26, 2018, https://hbr.org/2018/01/perfectionism-is-increasing-and-thats-not-good-news.

62   Patrick van Kessel, "How Americans Feel about the Satisfactions and Stresses of Modern Life," Pew Research Center (website), February 5, 2020, https://www.pewresearch.org/fact-tank/2020/02/05/how-americans-feel-about-the-satisfactions-and-stresses-of-modern-life/.

63   Wayne Muller, *Sabbath: Finding Rest, Renewal, and Delight in Our Busy Lives* (New York: Bantam, 1999), 2.

Part Two

Quote: David Platt, *Radical: Taking Back Your Faith from the American Dream* (Colorado Springs: Multnomah Books, 2010), 216–17.

Chapter 4

64   John 5:5.

65   John 5:6 (NIV).

66   John 5:7 (NIV).

67   *Encyclopaedia Britannica Online*, s.v. "carpe diem," accessed May 7, 2021, https://www.britannica.com/topic/carpe-diem.

68   Vocabulary.com, s.v. "significance," accessed September 20, 2021, https://www.vocabulary.com/dictionary/significance#.

69   Ken Blanchard, quoted in Lloyd Reeb, *From Success to Significance: When the Pursuit of Success Isn't Enough* (Grand Rapids: Zondervan, 2004), back cover.

70   Khalil Gibran, AZQuotes.com, *Wind and Fly LTD*, 2021, accessed on August 27, 2021, https://www.azquotes.com/quote/552449.

71   Proverbs 27:12 (NIV).

72   I hope this isn't weird, but I pray for you as I write each chapter of this book. I don't want you to miss your life. I know Jesus doesn't want that for you either. So I pray.

73   In some translations, you might find it as a footnote.

74   David Platt, *Radical: Taking Back Your Faith from the American Dream* (Colorado Springs: Multnomah Books, 2010), 7.

75   John 5:8 (NIV).

Chapter 5

76   Matthew 11:15 (NKJV).

77   Rick Warren, *The Purpose-Driven Life: What on Earth Am I Here for?* (Grand Rapids, MI: Zondervan, 2002), 17. *The Purpose Driven Life* spread like wild-fire across the world. Rick Warren didn't invent the concept, but he definitely struck a nerve.

78   Philippians 1:21 (NIV).

79   "Where Americans Find Meaning in Life," Pew Research Center, November 20, 2018, https://www.pewforum.org/2018/11/20/where-americans-find-meaning-in-life/.

80   John 10:10 (NIV).

81   John 6:35.

82   John 14:6 (NIV).

83   John 11:25 (NIV).

84   C. S. Lewis, *The Four Loves* (New York: Harcourt, Brace, 1960), 120.

85   Westminster Shorter Catechism, The Westminster Shorter Catechism Project (website), https://www.shortercatechism.com/.

86   Fyodor Dostoyevsky, *The Brothers Karamazov*, trans. Constance Garnett, (New York: Signet Classics, New American Library, 1912), 289.

87   Viktor E. Frankl, *Man's Search for Meaning*, trans. Ilse Lasch (London: Rider, An Imprint of Ebury Press, Random House, 2004), 84.

88   Luke 5:4 (NIV).

89   Luke 5:5 (NIV).

90   John 5:6 (NIV).

91   Vocabulary.com, s.v. "significance," accessed September 20, 2021, https://www.vocabulary.com/dictionary/significance#.

92   "Biblical vocabulary: the word הערכה (God's honor and glory)," *BiblWord*, a ministry of GlobalRize (website), August 27, 2020, https://www.biblword.net/biblical-vocabulary-gods-honor-and-glory-part-1/.

93   1 Corinthians 10:31 (NIV).

94   I wrote an entire book about this fan for the 2010 FIFA World Cup in South Africa. It's amazing that his little question could impact so many people, but the most amazing thing is, that fan read the book and wrote me a letter many years later. I'm still here, so I guess he wasn't mad.

95   Philippians 2:10 (NIV).

Chapter 6

96   Stephen Covey details this "funeral exercise" in his book, *The 7 Habits of Highly Effective People* (New York, NY: Simon & Schuster, 1989, 2004), 103–4. I try to work through this exercise annually. I've found it so beneficial to "begin with the end in mind."

97   Author unknown, but often attributed to Mother Teresa.

98   Virginia Durkin O'Shea, "Our Lenten Journey, March 5: Mother Teresa," *The Dialog* (website), Diocese of Wilmington, DE, April 5, 2020, https://thedialog.org/catechetical-corner/our-lenten-journey-march-5-mother-teresa/.

99   Wikipedia, s.v. "Missionaries of Charity," last modified August 29, 2021, 23:24, https://en.wikipedia.org/wiki/Missionaries_of_Charity.

100 "Profile: 'Living Saint' Mother Teresa," BBC News (website), December 18, 2015, https://www.bbc.com/news/world-asia-india-35130795.

101 Kenneth J. Cooper, "Solemn Farewell to Mother Teresa," *The Washington Post* (website), September 13, 1997, https://www.washingtonpost.com/archive/politics/1997/09/13/solemn-farewell-to-mother-teresa/8dfa7442-c726-4bc2-ad2b-9e2b5f75c014/.

102 Judges 17:6 (NLT).

103   Matthew 4:19 (NIV).

104   John 21:1–3 (NIV).

105   C. S. Lewis, *Mere Christianity* (London: Geoffrey Bles Ltd., 1952), 107.

106   Matthew 6:19–21 (NLT).

107   Steve Vernon, "How Do You Want to Be Remembered?" *Forbes*, February 19, 2019, https://www.forbes.com/sites/stevevernon/2019/02/19/how-do-you-want-to-be-remembered/?sh=169b94f3277f.

108   Bronnie Ware, *The Top Five Regrets of the Dying: A Life Transformed by the Dearly Departing* (Carlsbad, CA: Hay House Publishing, 2019); see also Bronnie Ware's website: https://bronnieware.com/regrets-of-the-dying/.

109   Often attributed to Mother Teresa.

110   Matthew 16:18 (NIV).

Intermission

111   Isaiah 40:6–7 (NIV).

112   Psalm 103:15–16 (ESV).

Part Three

Quote: Attributed to D. L. Moody.

Chapter 7

113   Dan Buettner, *The Blue Zones: 9 Lessons for Living Longer from the People Who've Lived the Longest* (Washington, DC: National Geographic Society, 2012), xxii.

114   Dan Buettner and Sam Skemp, "Blue Zones: Lessons from the World's Longest Lived," *American Journal of Lifestyle Medicine*, September/October 2016, https://www.ncbi.nlm.nih.gov/pmc/articles/PMC6125071/.

115   Buettern and Skemp, "Blue Zones."

116   Saint Augustine of Hippo, *The Confessions of Saint Augustine*, Translator: E. B. Pusey (Edward Bouverie) June, 2002 [EBook #3296], 3.

117   Warren, *The Purpose-Driven Life*, 30.

118   Matthew 6:33 (ESV).

119   Matthew 6:33 (MSG).

120   Gil Bailie, *Violence Unveiled: Humanity at the Crossroads* (New York: Crossroads Publishing Company, 1996), xv.

121   Matthew 22:2–5 (NIV).

122   John 15:16 (NIV).

123   John Mark Comer, *The Ruthless Elimination of Hurry* (New York: Crown Publishing Group, 2019), 159.

124   "Presidential Yacht Potomac: F. D. R.'s Floating White House," The Potomac Association (website), accessed September 25, 2021, https://www.usspotomac.org/history/. The ship changed hands several times after FDR's death and was eventually impounded when authorities discovered drug smugglers were using it as a front. The Potomac sat rotting in the East Bay Estuary in San Francisco and eventually sank.

125   Franklin Roosevelt, "Fireside Chat April 14, 1938," *The American Presidency Project* (website), accessed September 25, 2021, https://www.presidency.ucsb.edu/documents/fireside-chat-15.

126   D. A. Carson, *For the Love of God: A Daily Companion for Discovering the Riches of God's Word*, Vol. 2 (Wheaton, IL: Crossway, 2006), 23.

127   Ephesians 5:15 (NIV).

128   Matthew 7:21–23 (MSG).

129   Luke 12:16–18 (NIV).

130   Luke 12:20 (NIV).

131   Luke 12:20–21 (NIV).

132 Amy Watson, "Frequency of Reading the Bible among Adults in the United States from 2018 to 2021," Statista, last modified July 22, 2021, https://www.statista.com/statistics/299433/bible-readership-in-the-usa/.

133 Mark Clear, *Atomic Habits: A Full Simple Guide to Break Your Bad Routines and Learn New Good Ones* (New York: Avery, 2018), 38.

134 Mother Teresa, *A Simple Path*, compiled by Lucinda Vardey (New York: Ballantine Books, 1995), 79.

135 Malachi 3:10 (NIV).

136 William Blake, *The Prophetic Books of William Blake: Jerusalem, The Emanation of the Giant Albion* (1804), in the public domain, available for free download at https://www.google.com/books/edition/Jerusalem/h504AQAAMAAJ?hl=en&gbpv=1.

137 Alan Redpath, *Blessings out of Buffetings: Studies in Second Corinthians* (Grand Rapids, MI: F. H. Revell, 1993), 48.

Chapter 8

138 Danny Nettleton, "Dying of Thirst," *Ears to Hear* (blog), accessed September 25, 2021, https://eartstohear.wordpress.com/2015/09/08/dying-of-thirst/.

139 John Donne, "No Man is an Island," *The Works of John Donne Vol. III*. Henry Alford, ed. (London: John W. Parker, 1839), 574–5.

140 Timothy Keller, *The Reason for God: Belief in an Age of Skepticism* (London: Dutton, 2009), 216.

141 Genesis 2:18 (NIV).

142 Ecclesiastes 4:9–12 (NLT).

143 John 13:34.

144 Romans 12:10.

145 Romans 12:16.

146 Colossians 3:13.

147   Ephesians 4:32.

148   Romans 12:10 (ESV).

149   Brigham Young University, "Relationships Improve Your Odds of Survival by 50 Percent, Research Finds," *ScienceDaily* (website), July 28, 2010, https://www.sciencedaily.com/releases/2010/07/100727174909.htm.

150   The National Academies of Sciences, Engineering, and Medicine, "Social Isolation and Loneliness in Older Adults: Opportunities for the Health Care System," (Washington, DC: The National Academies Press, 2020), https://www.nap.edu/read/25663/chapter/1.

151   Louis J. Cozolino, *Timeless: Nature's Formula for Health and Longevity* (New York: W. W. Norton and Company, 2018), 110.

152   Monika Carless, "The Power of Vulnerability: Brené Brown's TED Talk May be the Breakthrough You've Been Looking For," *Elephant Journal*, Waylon H. Lewis Enterprises, February 27, 2017, https://www.elephantjournal.com/2017/02/power-vulnerability-brene-browns-ted-talk-may-be-the-breakthrough-youve-been-looking-for/.

153   Hebrews 10:24–25 (NIV).

154   Proverbs 27:17 (NIV).

155   Matthew 6:9–13 (NIV).

156   John Wesley, "Sermon 24, Upon Our Lord's Sermon on the Mount, Discourse 4," Sermons on Several Occasions, accessed November 22, 2021, https://www.ccel.org/ccel/wesley/sermons.v.xxiv.html.

157   Nirmita Panchal, Rabah Kamal, Cynthia Cox, "The Implications of COVID-19 for Mental Health and Substance Use," *KFF*, Kaiser Family Foundation, February 10, 2021, https://www.kff.org/coronavirus-covid-19/issue-brief/the-implications-of-covid-19-for-mental-health-and-substance-use/.

158   Proverbs 18:1 (ESV).

159   Matthew 11:28–30 (MSG).

160   Timothy Paul Jones, *Finding God in a Galaxy Far, Far Away: A Spiritual Exploration of the Star Wars Saga* (Colorado Springs: Multnomah Books, 2005), 71.

161   Rob Cross, "To Be Happier at Work, Invest More in Your Relationships," *Harvard Business Review*, July 30, 2019, https://hbr.org/2019/07/to-be-happier-at-work-invest-more-in-your-relationships.

162   Dr. Emma Seppala, "Connectedness and Health: The Science of Social Connection," The Center for Compassion and Altruism Research and Education, Stanford Medicine, May 8, 2014, http://ccare.stanford.edu/uncategorized/connectedness-health-the-science-of-social-connection-infographic/.

Chapter 9

163   Prakash Iyer, "Gandhi and The One Shoe Syndrome," Prakash Iyer (blog), *Medium*, October 2, 2016, https://medium.com/@prakashiyer/gandhi-and-the-one-shoe-syndrome-3567a4962cb6.

164   Robert Forbes, "My Father, Malcolm Forbes: A Never-Ending Adventure," *Forbes* (website), August 19. 2019, https://www.forbes.com/sites/forbesdigitalcovers/2019/08/19/my-father-malcolm-forbes-a-never-ending-adventure/?sh=2d1da77219fb.

165   Abram Brown, "Jewels, Eggs and Empires: The Story Of Forbes And Faberge," *Forbes* (website), September 19, 2017, https://www.forbes.com/sites/abrambrown/2017/09/19/forbes-faberge/?sh=3eaf1bcd4ccf.

166   Winston Churchill Quotes, *BrainyQuote.com*, BrainyMedia Inc, 2021, accessed August 30, 2021, https://www.brainyquote.com/quotes/winston_churchill_131192.

167   Ashoka, "12 Great Quotes from Gandhi on His Birthday," *Forbes* (website), October 2, 2012, https://www.forbes.com/sites/ashoka/2012/10/02/12-great-quotes-from-gandhi-on-his-birthday/?sh=1eb60d3833d8.

168   Jenny Santi, *The Giving Way to Happiness: Stories and Science behind the Life-Changing Power of Giving* (New York: Penguin Publishing Group, 2016), 7–8.

169   Proverbs 11:24–25 (NIV).

170   Bible Study Tools, s.v. "dashen," accessed September 27, 2021, https://www.biblestudytools.com/lexicons/hebrew/kjv/dashen.html.

171   Proverbs 11:24 (MSG).

172   Matthew 13:12 (NIV).

173   Christian Smith and Hilary Davidson, *The Paradox of Generosity: Giving We Receive, Grasping We Lose* (New York: Oxford University Press, 2014), 1.

174   John 3:16 (NIV).

175   Romans 8:32 (NIV).

176   John 10:10 (NLT).

177   Malachi 3:10 (NIV).

178   Zig Ziglar, *Secrets of Closing the Sale* (Ada, MI: Baker Publishing Group, 2019), 22.

179   "Ask Not What Your People Can Do for You," The John Maxwell Company (website), June 2, 2014, https://www.johnmaxwell.com/blog/ask-not-what-your-people-can-do-for-you/.

180   "57 Famous Pablo Picasso Quotes About Life (ART)," Gracious (website), January 23, 2021, https://graciousquotes.com/picasso/.

181   Allan Luks and Peggy Payne, *The Healing Power of Doing Good: The Health and Spiritual Benefits of Helping Others* (Lincoln, NE: iUniverse, 2001), 126.

182   Jorge Moll et al., "Human fronto-mesolimbic networks guide decisions about charitable donation," Proceedings of the National Academy of Sciences of the United States of America, vol. 103.42 (October 2006).

183   Caitlin Fairchild, "Performing Random Acts of Kindness Can Make You Happier," The Renewal Project (website), Allstate, January 13, 2020, https://www.therenewalproject.com/one-easy-way-to-be-happier-from-a-psychologist-who-studies-human-happiness/.

184 Stephen Garrard Post and Jill Neimark, *Why Good Things Happen to Good People: How to Live a Longer, Healthier, Happier Life by the Simple Act of Giving* (New York: Broadway Books, 2008), 55–58.

185 Doug Oman, Carl Thoresen, and Kay Mcmahon, "Volunteerism and Mortality among the Community-dwelling Elderly," *Journal of Health Psychology*, Vol. 4. 301–16, doi: 10.1177/135910539900400301.

186 Jenny Santi, *The Giving Way to Happiness*, 28.

187 Barbara Fredrickson, *Positivity: Top-Notch Research Reveals the 3-to-1 Ratio That Will Change Your Life* (New York: Harmony Rodale Books, 2009), 128.

188 James H. Fowler and Nicholas A. Christakis, "Cooperative Behavior Cascades in Human Social Networks," Proceedings of the National Academy of Sciences (March 2010), https://www. pnas.org/content/107/12/5334.

189 Fowler and Christakis, "Cooperative Behavior."

190 Rusty Rustenbach, "Giving Yourself Away: Servanthood," *Discipleship Journal*, Campus Christian Ministry (website), 1985, http://www.campuschristians.info/reading-library/ giving-yourself-away-servanthood/.

Epilogue

191 Henri J. M. Nouwen, *Here and Now: Living in the Spirit* (New York: Crossroads, 1994), 131.

192 Mark 8:36 (MSG).

193 Henry David Thoreau, *Walden; or Life in the Woods* (Boston: Houghton Mifflin, 2007), 143.

194 James Strong, "perissoj," in *Strong's Greek Hebrew Dictionary*, accessed September 27, 2021, http://www.godrules.net/library/ strongs2b/gre4053.htm.